GETTING RICH WITH REIT INVESTING

A BEGINNER'S GUIDE TO GETTING STARTED WITH LOW CAPITAL TO GENERATE WEALTH FROM REAL ESTATE WITHOUT OWNING PHYSICAL PROPERTY

ROMAN STERLING

Copyright © 2023 by Roman Sterling

All rights reserved.

No part of this book may be reproduced in any form or by any electronic or mechanical means, including information storage and retrieval systems, without written permission from the author, except for the use of brief quotations in a book review. It is illegal to copy this book, post it to a website, or distribute it by any other means without permission.

This publication is designed to provide accurate and authoritative information in regard to the subject matter covered. It is sold with the understanding that the author is not engaged in rendering legal, investment, accounting or other professional services. While the author has used their best efforts in preparing this book, they make no representations or warranties with respect to the accuracy or completeness of the contents of this book and specifically disclaim any implied warranties of merchantability or fitness for a particular purpose. No warranty may be created or extended by sales representatives or written sales materials. The advice and strategies contained herein may not be suitable for your situation. You should consult with a professional when appropriate. The author shall not be liable for any monetary loss, damages, reparation, or any other commercial damages, including but not limited to special, incidental, consequential, personal, or other damages, due to the information contained within this book, either directly or indirectly.

The author has no responsibility for the persistence or accuracy of URLs for external or third-party Internet Websites referred to in this publication and does not guarantee that any content on such Websites is, or will remain, accurate or appropriate.

First edition.

Disclaimer Notice:

The following work is for informational and educational purposes only. None of the information herein constitues an offer to sell or buy any security or investment vehicle, nor does it constitue an investment recommendation of a legal, tax, accounting or investment recommendation by the author. The information is presented without regard for individual investment preferences or risk parameters and is general, non-tailored, non-specific information. Always consult a professional for investment, legal, tax and accounting advice.

CONTENTS

Introduction — vii

1. WHY REITS ARE WORTH YOUR TIME (AND MONEY) — 1
   - Why Invest In Real Estate? — 2
   - REITs In A Nutshell — 5
   - How Do REITs Work? — 8
   - REITs vs Other Investments — 9
   - REITs vs Physical Real Estate — 10

2. TYPES OF REITS TO KNOW — 12
   - A Brief History — 12
   - How the SEC Defines REITs — 13
   - The Different Types of REITs — 14
   - Other Types Of REITs — 21
   - The Right REIT For You — 23

3. THE NO-BS BLUEPRINT FOR REIT INVESTING — 26
   - Step 1: Figure Out What You Want — 27
   - Step 2: Determine Your Budget — 28
   - Step 3: Research — 30
   - Step 4: Evaluate and Score — 31

4. SCREENING AND EVALUATING REITS — 33
   - What To Look For When Filtering Through REITs — 34
   - Step 1: Dividend Yield — 35
   - Step 2: Return on Equity (ROE) — 36
   - Step 3: Price-To-Book Ratio (P/B) — 37
   - Step 4: Funds-from-Operations (FFO) & Earnings-Per-Share (EPS) — 37
   - Step 5: Debt-To-Equity (D/E) Ratio — 38
   - How to Use a Screener — 39
   - Step 6: How To Analyze A REIT's Management Team — 41

Choosing Your REIT	44
Investing In Your REIT	45
Dividend Reinvestment Plan (DRIP)	46
5. INVESTING IN PUBLICLY TRADED REITS	48
Pros & Cons	49
The Pros	50
The Cons	51
How To Invest In Publicly Traded REITs	53
Best Practices	56
6. INVESTING IN NON-TRADED REITS	59
Private REITs	60
PNLR (Public Non-Listed REIT)	60
Similarities & Differences	61
Pros & Cons	62
How To Invest In A Non-Traded REIT	64
7. REIT INVESTING ON A BUDGET	67
Low-Cost REIT Investment Options	68
Expense Ratios	71
Popular REIT ETFs	71
Pros & Cons Of REIT ETFs	73
Real Estate Crowdfunding: The New Kid On The Block	75
Fractional Shares	76
8. HOW TO MINIMIZE YOUR TAX BURDEN	78
How REITS Are Taxed	79
The Tax Advantages Of REITs	80
9. THE RISKY SIDE OF REIT INVESTING	83
The Risks	84
10. DOS AND DON'TS OF REIT INVESTING	88
11. ADVANCED REIT STRATEGIES	93
REIT Option Trading	93
200-Day Moving Average	96
Using Leverage	98
Relationship to Your Existing Investments	99

12. CONCLUSION	100
References	103

INTRODUCTION

Buy a house, fix it up, rent it out, sell it. That's what most people think real estate investing is. And at the surface level, they would be right; but they don't see everything else that comes along with it, which is why I want to begin this book with a horror story. By the time you've finished reading it, you might discover real estate investing is not all it's cracked up to be.

If there is one thing I hated nothing more as a real estate investor, it was terrible tenants. Specifically, the ones that would leave a horrible mess and then vacate without notice, which is precisely what happened to me with one of my last investment properties.

We're talking about cigarette burns on the furniture, holes in the walls, rotting food, old newspapers covering the floor, and pet waste everywhere. Not to mention, there were bed bugs and other pests - the sight itself would make your skin crawl. It was like a scene from a horror movie, except this was real life. I was doing everything I could to not scream at the horrifying sight before my eyes.

Around this time, I was selling all my property to other

investors, and this was the last one on the list. It took me months and thousands of dollars to fix the place up before it finally switched hands. Let me tell you, I have never been so relieved to sell a property.

Sure, you can make plenty of money investing in real estate, but it takes a lot of work. I didn't mind the buying and selling process; that part was fun. But dealing with unruly tenants that break things, make noise and don't clean up after themselves can be exhausting. And when it comes to tracking down tenants that are behind on rent, you better have a deep reservoir of patience.

Dealing with day-to-day issues and maintenance is also a time-consuming and often never-ending process. Not to mention the larger issues that inevitably appear, like water damage, permit delays, and dealing with unreliable contractors, just to name a few.

I love real estate. I can talk about it all day until I'm blue in the face, but I wanted to find a way to continue investing in it without sacrificing my sanity. Enough was enough.

I was at dinner one night during a real estate conference, and sitting to my right was a colleague I had gotten to know over the years. I vented my frustrations about real estate investing to them, and that's when they told me about a different approach. They explained that I could keep a portfolio of properties without any of the hassles, like unruly tenants and maintenance. They were talking about Real Estate Investment Trusts, or REITs for short.

From that moment on, I wanted to learn everything I could.

After dinner, I returned to my hotel room and opened my laptop. I googled myself down a rabbit hole that led me to read plenty of articles, blog posts and forums. I was scribbling notes down like a madman. Hours passed, and I needed sleep for my flight home that was fast approaching, so I called it a night.

When I returned home, I continued to dive deeper into REITs. I even asked people in my network about them and picked their brains as much as possible. I couldn't believe what I was learning and wanted to share it with as many people as possible, which led to me writing this book.

WHAT ARE REITS (AND WHAT MAKES IT DIFFERENT FROM DIRECT INVESTING)?

As mentioned, REITs are Real Estate Investment Trusts. They allow you to invest in large-scale real estate operations that generate income and financial growth. This is the perfect way for an individual investor (possibly yourself) to earn a share of the income and financial growth produced from that real estate.

Here's the cool part: you don't need to go through the process of acquiring physical real estate. You don't need to search for specific properties, put in an offer, or apply for a loan, and you can still benefit from the real estate market.

Is it sinking in yet?

At this point, you might be thinking, "Where was this when I initially thought about real estate investing?" I was the same way when I started learning about the benefits of REITs.

WHAT WILL YOU LEARN IN THIS BOOK?

If you're reading this book, it tells me you are interested in investing. You might have considered the idea of investing in real estate, or perhaps you've heard about REITs in passing and want to learn more.

In this book, you will learn the ins and outs of REITs and why they are a great alternative to physical real estate. You'll learn my no-BS blueprint to help you choose the best REIT for your portfolio and financial goals. Finding a solid REIT can be challenging, but I will make the process as simple as possible for you.

I've used my 15+ years of real estate and investing experience to write a book that will give you the information and tools needed to make sound REIT investing decisions. Along with the valuable information in this book will be actionable steps you can take today. You will learn a step-by-step process on how to use REITs to achieve your financial goals. But remember, if you skip steps or cut corners, you won't be able to achieve the success you want.

WHO IS THIS BOOK FOR?

This book is for anyone interested in investing in real estate using a different approach. You may want to supplement your income to have more financial freedom. Or perhaps you're starting to think about how you will fund your retirement. There is no harm in considering investing for retirement if you are in your 20s, 30s, or 40s. When that day comes, you will need an income source, and REITs can help.

However, whatever your goal is, you have to understand that this won't make you rich overnight. REITs can build wealth over time, but it takes patience and consistency.

Look at Sam Zell, the billionaire who is considered the forefather of REITs. Sam had a history of turning distressed properties into valuable ones, but he's known for making REITs what they are today: a wealth-building vehicle for those interested in real estate but don't want to "get their hands dirty." He knew how tough it was to maintain properties, so he created something for others to invest in that gave the benefits of property ownership without the pitfalls. He used REITs to turn himself into a real estate powerhouse, but it didn't happen overnight. It happened over the span of his 50+ year career. Sam, and other billionaires like him, know the power of REITs and swear by them.

Now, you might be saying, "50 years is way too long!" The good news is, unless you're aiming to be a billionaire, achieving your REIT investing goals won't take 50 years.

BEFORE WE BEGIN...ONE LAST THING

If you expect this to be a get-rich-quick scheme, I encourage you to put down the book and don't pick it up again until you understand that investing and building wealth is a long-term process.

This book is for those who are aware of what investing entails. It's not some casino game where you risk it all and let it ride. You need to make the right moves using the right strategies. I encourage you to read this book carefully. Highlight key points and take notes.

On that note, it's time to get started. Turn to the next page, and we'll begin Chapter 1.

[Financial Disclaimer: Please note that I am not a financial advisor. The information in this book should not be mistaken for financial advice. If you require professional advice, seek the assistance of a financial advisor - especially someone who knows about REITs. Also, keep in mind that with all investing opportunities, risks exist. I also would be remiss if I didn't mention this one key aspect of investing - doing your due diligence.]

CHAPTER 1
WHY REITS ARE WORTH YOUR TIME (AND MONEY)

"The biggest risk of all is not taking one."

MELODY HOBSON

There are two things people worry and complain about when they think about investing in real estate: 1) It takes a lot of upfront capital, and 2) It requires expertise.

When it comes to the amount of money you need to invest in real estate, it is no surprise to hear that many people believe you need thousands - if not hundreds of thousands - of dollars to make an investment that will count.

The other assumption that nearly everyone makes when thinking about investing in real estate is they believe you have to be an expert if you want to make a sizable impact on the market. If you're going to find the right property, pay the right price, and then convert it into the right sort of financial gain, you need to be an expert. Many people think this to be true, but it's not accurate.

Instead, the truth is that you can make money investing in real estate even if you aren't putting your life savings into it. You can also do a lot without being an expert in the field. You don't need both of these things to be a talented, successful, and financially stable real estate investor.

Now, sometimes you do need piles of money and expertise to make a splash in certain parts of the real estate market. But with REITs, you can dip your toes into real estate without losing your shirt. For many people, they are a great way to discover the world of real estate investing at a fraction of the cost. Of course, that means that REITs attract many people who have never invested in real estate - or anything - before. Therefore, you need to learn about and understand them. No, you don't have to be an expert in real estate to find great success in REITs. You do, however, need to learn about this specific, special kind of investment.

So, what are REITs, and what makes them so attractive? Why is this the approach you should take when you are dipping your toes, at least for now, in real estate investing?

WHY INVEST IN REAL ESTATE?

Let's start by talking about why people invest in real estate in the first place.

You should invest your money in the real estate market for plenty of reasons. In fact, you might have heard people say that real estate investing is, at times, as close as you can get to a sure thing. If you are careful about how you invest, you can enjoy a strong cash flow and excellent returns. That is because people always need places to live and places to establish businesses. There are also many advantages regarding taxes.

GETTING RICH WITH REIT INVESTING 3

I'm sure you have heard about plenty of people who made their fortunes - or even just a sizable supplemental income - in real estate. What is it that draws them in? Let's consider the biggest reasons why you should invest in real estate.

Cash Flow

The net income you get from your real estate investment after you make your mortgage payments and expenses is called your cash flow. What causes your cash flow? The most significant source is if you rent out the space you own or invest in.

If you want to make any real estate investment worth your time and money, you need to generate a strong cash flow. The good news is that the cash flow will grow stronger over time.

Tax Breaks

If you take your real estate investments seriously, you'll know there are plenty of tax breaks and deductions you can use to make your investment worth it. You can take advantage of many different breaks in the tax code and deductions that will save you a lot of money at the end of the financial year when tax time rolls around.

Some of the deductions you can make money from involve the cost of operating, managing, and owning your property. And those are just some of them. There are plenty more ways to deduct from your taxes and experience big breaks that will make owning and investing in real estate all the more attractive.

Appreciation

Here is one of the biggest reasons someone new to investing will want to put their money and time into real estate: appreciation is very real and can add a lot to your bottom line.

Appreciation is the price and value of property improving over time. Real estate values tend to increase over time, and if you strike when the iron is hot, you will see the value of the place that you own or invest in only go up, up, up over the years. This will allow you to charge more when it comes to residents or businesses leasing or renting from you. As the appreciation of your investment grows, so does the amount of money you receive from it.

Diversification

The thing about investing is that it always comes with risk. There is simply no sure thing when it comes to investing. This is true for people who invest in cryptocurrency, commodities, companies, and the real estate market. If you are looking for a way to make money without taking a risk, you shouldn't invest.

But here is the thing: investing in the real estate market is a great way to lessen the risks. That is because investing in real estate is a great way to diversify your portfolio. Diversifying is the act of making sure that you are investing in multiple things at one time. To be more precise, you're not putting all your eggs in one basket. This will help avoid the volatile moments markets experience and will help keep your investments and money safe. Well, as safe as possible, anyway.

Despite all the advantages of real estate investing, there are still disadvantages. That is just the plain and honest truth, and it's unavoidable for any type of investing. Lack of cash is one of the key drawbacks when it comes to the real estate market. Additionally, a real estate deal may take months to finalize, as opposed to a stock or bond deal, which may be finished in seconds. Finding the ideal counterparty might take many weeks of labor, even with a broker's assistance.

However, real estate is a unique asset class with a clear risk-return profile that may improve an investor's portfolio. It is also a straightforward and relatively simple type of asset. Real estate provides cash flow, tax benefits, and price appreciation. Additionally, real estate may improve a portfolio by reducing volatility via diversity.

So, now you know why you should be toying with the idea of investing in the real estate market. Now it is time to dig into REITs, an excellent way to put just a bit of money into the market and make a huge splash.

REITS IN A NUTSHELL

There are typically three types of real estate investors.

Some people buy just one piece of property. They might move their family into it, renovate it, live there for years, and then sell the house decades later when the appreciation has grown so much that they profit from it. You might have seen this happen to friends or family, or even experienced it yourself. But few people consider buying a home as an investment. Instead, they think of it as a place to live and raise their families. The thing is, real estate is always an investment that can make you cash in the long run.

Others invest in multiple properties. Sure, they may live in one of the properties, but they can rent out or lease the others. This is a form of passive income that can make a huge difference in someone's life. People can earn thousands of dollars annually by investing in multiple real estate properties.

Then there are companies whose purpose is to find properties, invest in them, and turn a profit. They can do this by studying the market, the location, and the community's needs. Does a particular area call for a complex that can house businesses? Maybe the region needs more housing for lower-income families. Or perhaps it's great for farming or land development. There are, in fact, many ways that buying property can turn into a successful venture. Numerous companies now make millions by knowing what the people around them need and giving it to them via well-placed property.

That last investor type is a very important one because it perfectly ties into REITs. In the simplest ways, a REIT is a lot like a mutual fund. More specifically, an equity mutual fund. Now, what is an equity mutual fund? That is important to know if you are trying to figure out how REITs can appeal to you.

An equity mutual fund is something that many first-time investors put their money into because it is an easier way to invest in multiple things at once. Instead of browsing the stock market, doing a ton of research, and settling on the companies you want to invest in, an equity mutual fund lets you select a fund manager who will do all that work for you. And instead of choosing just one stock to invest in, this manager will select a portfolio of them. You don't have to do the hard work of picking and choosing your investments. Instead, your job is to find the right manager to determine the perfect equity mutual fund for you.

A REIT is like an equity mutual fund. It is a collection of properties controlled, owned, and operated by a professional management team you can invest in. You are investing in the property to a degree, but you are also investing in the management team. You are finding a group that says the right things, has the right vision, and gains your trust. You are placing your hard-earned money in them, their plans, and their strategy.

As you can imagine, the benefits of investing in a REIT are plenty. The biggest is that you can make significant profits with a fairly reasonable investment. You don't have to invest millions of dollars to get good results.

Plus, a REIT can help you diversify your portfolio. What happens if you put all your money into just one piece of property? Maybe it's a very promising property, but what if it doesn't start returning on your investment? What if the neighborhood goes down the tubes, or there is a disaster, or it just can't seem to keep residents in it for one reason or another? That means all the money you have sunk into this pit won't be worth it. With a REIT, you can avoid some of those risks because you are investing in multiple properties at the same time.

Additionally, investing in a REIT means that you are investing in experts. The managers who run these trusts are professionals trained in the market and carry excellent knowledge into every choice they make. They know what to look for in the best markets and the worst. They remember critical facts and tiny details; they understand the entire industry better than anyone else. Plus, they *want* you to do well. They get paid more if your investment takes off. Why wouldn't they want it to succeed? It will only help their bottom line and their profile among investors.

One of the best things about putting your money into a REIT is that you can be very specific about the sector you want to place your cash in.

REITs are generally made to specialize and focus on a particular kind of real estate. For example, REITs can be centered around multi-family housing, inner-city apartments, or luxury condos. They also cater to office buildings and even cell phone towers and farmland.

Therefore, as an example, if you are an investor who believes in the future of low-income housing, you can find a REIT specializing in that. Not only can you invest in a team of professionals, but also a cause you believe in.

For many reasons, REITs are one of the best and most innovative ways for people of all types, especially newcomers, to invest in the real estate market.

HOW DO REITS WORK?

We have already discussed how REITs work in principle, but there are a few more things to remember.

As mentioned, they are usually set up to specialize in a specific sector or industry. From inner-city dwellings to businesses to restaurants and more, REITs allow investors to put their money into a particular sector or housing accommodation.

Another thing to remember about the workings of a REIT is that the law requires that 90% of its profits go to the shareholders (investors) in the form of dividends. That is an excellent thing to know, and it promises that the vast majority of money made by a REIT will go to the people who invest in it, not the team or CEO behind it.

Something else to know is at least 75% of the total assets must be comprised of real estate, and at least 75% of the company's income must come from that rental portfolio.

More importantly, at least 100 shareholders must be involved in the REIT, with no more than 50% of the total shares held by five or fewer investors. This is one of the trickiest parts of running a REIT because it can sometimes take a lot of work to drum up support from 100 shareholders. But this is required by law, and so many REITs never get off the ground.

The bottom line about the inner workings of a REIT is that

instead of owning real estate, you instead own a share of the company that owns the real estate. It's like investing in a company and making money based on its performance instead of buying, owning, selling, and managing your own properties.

If you believe in a company, why not let them make the money for you? That is the general principle behind REITs, and it has worked very well for many people.

REITS VS OTHER INVESTMENTS

You may wonder about the difference between investing in REITs and stocks. If you want to decide if REITs are right for you, you need to know the difference between the two.

It is important to remember that both REITs and more traditional stock investments will come with volatility. You'll experience ups and downs in the market, and you can't get around that.

However, REITs are usually better for many investors because they tend to experience *less* volatility. This is because the real estate market moves much slower than other markets. Plus, REITs tend to outperform stocks on the whole. A stock can rise - and fall - in price in a matter of hours, which can scare investors away. And when investors flee, the value of the stock will drop in a short amount of time. But people stick with REITs long-term more often; therefore, their value is usually higher, which is why they are seen as outperforming other stocks and investments.

At the same time, you may see a faster return on your investment when you put your money into more traditional stocks and commodities. As mentioned, the real estate market doesn't move as quickly. Therefore, if you want an investment that will pay you back as soon as possible, you might not be happy with a REIT. You can get a sizable return on your investment with great cash flow along the way, but it may take a bit more time. Investing in REITs will be a practice of patience for you, but since there is typically less volatility compared to stocks and other investments, you can rest easier knowing that it will pay off in the long run.

One last difference is the cash flow generated by REITs. REITs are known for their healthy, steady dividends, which are attractive to many people. Having a stream of reliable income every month can provide you with more financial security at any stage of life.

REITS VS PHYSICAL REAL ESTATE

What is the difference between investing in a REIT or physical real estate? Why not just buy a property to dive into the real estate market? What advantages and differences come with REITs instead? We've discussed a few already, but let's go into more detail.

For starters, putting your money into a REIT is far less hassle. Remember, you are not doing all the legwork to find the right investment properties. Instead, you are handing your money to a team of professionals who will do everything for you. Less hassle is a big, enticing draw for many people who don't want to get bogged down with the day-to-day problems of physical real estate. Remember the horror story I shared with you earlier? With REITs, you don't have to deal with any of that!

You also don't have to spend as much when you are buying into a REIT. When you invest your money in an actual piece of property, you will have to spend thousands of dollars upfront. But with a REIT, you will be paying much less. You won't be the sole owner of the property, but the smaller entry point is a great draw and a massive benefit. You can get started with as little, or as much as you want. Want to start with $100? Done. Want to throw in a few thousand? Sure. Whatever starting capital you have, you can make it work.

And of course, you have less risk with a REIT. Now, some people might say more risk equals more reward, which can be true. But if you play your cards right, the payoff from REITs can be incredible. I'll talk more later on about how to pick the right REITs and formulate a plan that will help you create long-term success.

In the end, many benefits come with investing in a REIT; appreciation is one of them, diversification is another, ease of use, predictability, and the lack of volatility are just a few more.

Overall, REITs are an excellent way for a first time investor to try their hand at the real estate market. It's also a great way for a seasoned investor to find a new way to make money. Whether you have been doing this a long time or are new to the game, the upsides always outweigh the downsides.

But you can only set yourself up for success in REIT investing if you learn some important characteristics. For example, did you know there are different categories of REITs? I'm not referring to the type of property they invest in. There are varied classifications of REITs, and the more you know, the better.

Luckily, the next chapter will explain everything you need to know about the various REIT types waiting for you.

CHAPTER 2
TYPES OF REITS TO KNOW

"For the best return on your money, pour your purse into your head."

BENJAMIN FRANKLIN

A BRIEF HISTORY

As mentioned before, REITs have a particular offering for investors who wish to buy into them.

When you put your money into a REIT, you place it in real estate of a unique type. You are investing in restaurants, low-income housing, typical residential, and much more.

But there is much more to REITs than just that.

For example, did you know they have been around since the 1960s when Congress established them as a way to allow Americans the chance to invest in income-producing real estate? They had seen the success the aforementioned mutual funds had provided citizens, and they wanted to allow them access to more financial windfalls.

Since then, the popularity of REITs and the prosperity that comes with them has exploded. Investing is now more accessible than ever for average Americans and people around the world who don't have much experience in this realm and don't want the commitment of devoting their life to it.

Did you know the number of jobs REITs create is immense and critical to the US economy? In 2021 alone, more than 3 million jobs and $225 billion in labor income were created by REITs. About 45% of the entire United States population lives in a home owned by REITs. They are more common than you think and beneficial to many Americans. It's no wonder that more than 40 countries worldwide have adopted the concept of REITs. People from all over the globe have seen the financial windfalls they have brought Americans, and they want in on it.

REITs are only growing in popularity. But why? Well, mainly because physical property will always be needed. No matter the economic problems or current events, businesses and people will need a place to reside. Therefore, REITs will always be attached to an industry that is forever in use and necessary to society. They will never go out of style. All investors need to do is be savvy about finding the right REIT at the right time. If you can understand the market, the industry, the people, and their desires and trends, you can capitalize on that and make some serious money by choosing the preferred REIT for you.

HOW THE SEC DEFINES REITS

According to the SEC, a REIT is "a company that owns – and typically operates – income-producing real estate or real estate-related assets." But of course, there is much more to them than just that.

To be qualified as a REIT, the company in question has to have at least 75% of its assets and income related to real estate investments and also, as mentioned before, distribute at least 90 percent of its income to shareholders annually. Additionally, no more than 25 percent of its assets can consist of non-qualifying securities or stock-taxable REIT subsidiaries. It must also be managed by a board of directors or trustees.

That is all a bunch of government-speak that comes down to this: a REIT needs to revolve around real estate in multiple ways and pay back the vast majority of profits to the shareholders.

Now that you have some background on REITs, let's talk about the different ways REITs can be structured.

THE DIFFERENT TYPES OF REITS

When starting your investing journey, you need to be aware of the three types of REITs: Mortgage, Equity, and Hybrid. Depending on your investing goals, one type of REIT may be better for you than another.

Equity REITs are very prominent, so let's start with them. When you hear someone speak about a REIT, they are most likely talking about an equity REIT.

Equity REITs

Equity REITs are real estate firms that control and oversee income-generating real estate, such as office buildings, malls, and apartment complexes, with the income being generated from tenants. There is a good chance that you have visited or spent money in an establishment tied to, and a part of, an equity REIT.

Like all other REITs, equity REITs distribute most of their yearly profits as dividends to their shareholders after covering operational costs for their properties. Equity REITs make money from the sale of assets as well.

It is easy to understand why most REITs fall into the equity category. There will forever be a need for retail space, apartment complexes, and single-family homes. The fact that properties in equity REITs can make a profit by their very existence makes this type of REIT very attractive to investors.

Congress used an intentionally vague definition of real estate when crafting the original REIT law decades ago since it recognized that the function and applications of real estate in a growing economy would evolve in tandem with economic development and changing technologies. They left a lot of wiggle room in their definition, leading to the importance, power, and prominence of equity REITs.

Because of this, equity REITs control properties connected to practically every sector of the economy, including those where we reside, do business and spend our free time. Apartments, shopping complexes, hotels, storage units, hospitals, nursing homes, data centers, and telecommunication towers are just a few of the types of real estate that equity REITs possess.

Think of how those sorts of locations impact and help your life every day. Do you live in an apartment? Do you often stay at hotels? Do you keep some family heirlooms in a storage unit business, or have you ever been to a hospital? Surely, you have a cell phone and rely on a phone tower to make your calls.

As you can see, the sort of real estate connected to equity REITs is essential for the ongoing economy and financial well-being of the United States and every other country in the world. Therefore, investing in an equity REIT is investing in real estate that keeps the world turning.

In order to fund projects that regenerate communities, allow digital commerce to power essential community services, and create future infrastructure, raising funds is necessary. REITs are an excellent method to do this while also generating economic activity and employment in the United States and other countries.

Historically, equity REITs have outperformed other REIT types on a total-return basis. That means they have provided the best long-term results compared to other REIT types. Equity REITs also provide relatively stable dividend income.

With such an upside and positive impact on the world, why wouldn't someone want to invest in an equity REIT? There are a few reasons.

For starters, there are countless options to choose from. Being the most popular means the sheer selection of choices could be overwhelming. You may not know where to start, and that could be enough to make you hesitant. However, I'll show you a quick and reliable way to create a shortlist of potential REITs to invest in that will make the decision much easier for you.

Some people may also be morally opposed to profiting from charging someone rent for shelter. Additionally, others are not a fan of equity REITs because their strength and well-being rely on the market. Equity REITs are related to commerce, so if the economy is suffering or a specific sector isn't doing well, they can suffer.

Although REITs are more secure and less volatile than other investment types, they are not without their risks. They, too, have their good times and bad, their ups and downs. There is no sure thing in any type of investing, and although REIT income and price growth can never be guaranteed, it can be stable compared to other investments.

· · ·

Mortgage REITs

Let's move on to the next type of REIT: the mortgage REIT. While not as popular as equity REITs, there are many upsides to investing in them.

Most real estate is associated with mortgages, the loan given to a business, person, or family buying a property. As you have surely expected, mortgage REITs are investment trusts specializing in mortgages, mortgage-backed securities, or related assets.

The big difference between equity and mortgage REITs is that the latter don't make their money by owning, managing, or developing properties like apartment complexes or retail locations. Instead, they profit based solely on the interest they charge for providing these loans to real estate locations. Think of it as investing in a lender. They can leverage considerable amounts of debt to earn their revenue in the form of interest.

Why would someone want to put their money into a mortgage REIT rather than an equity one? Well, if you're opposed to the ups and downs of the market, you can still do quite well if you have your cash in a mortgage REIT. That is because mortgages are being paid even when companies aren't buying new locations. If the economy slows, in other words, people and businesses still have to pay their mortgages.

There will be times when the economy comes to a crawl, and a slowdown can affect how many people buy homes or businesses open locations. But even when this happens, you can still make decent money via your mortgage REIT. Equity REITs might give you a more stable income; however, mortgage REITs often grant you a higher dividend yield.

Something else to consider is interest rates. Mortgage REITs are highly sensitive to interest rate changes. They can perform better or worse when rates fluctuate. Naturally, if interest rates rise, most people think that is good for a mortgage REIT since they would be receiving larger interest rate payments. But we need to take short-term, and long-term rates into consideration.

Mortgage REITs use debt to fund their operations. Some borrow up to 85% of their market value of assets! When they borrow money, they usually have a 6-month term associated with their debt. That means they are paying a particular interest rate for 6-months, which falls into the short-term interest rate category. The mortgages they have as assets, however, typically have long-term interest rates, such as 2-5 years. If the interest rate on the mortgage REIT's debt is lower than the interest rates on their income generating assets, they make money. But what if rates start to rise and short-term rates rise quicker than long-term rates? The income earned will get smaller and smaller over time, decreasing the dividends going into your pocket. This will also negatively affect the REIT's share price eventually.

However, what happens if long-term rates rise quicker than short-term rates? In that case, a mortgage REIT's cash flows will strengthen, profitability will grow, and the dividends going into your pocket become more secure. This will also attract more investors, which will inevitably increase the share price.

The reverse of those scenarios can happen when interest rates are decreasing as well.

So, if a mortgage REIT can be affected positively or negatively by fluctuating rates, how do you know which one to buy? Well, that takes a bit more effort to figure out. You'll need to do much more research to determine how a particular mortgage REIT will be affected in different interest rate environments by looking at their financials.

The best kinds of mortgage REITs to own are those that do well in a rising rate environment. More specifically, if you can determine that they have a fixed rate on their debt obligations, but most of their assets have variable rates attached to them, that is a winning combination in a rising rate environment. The mortgage REITs rate will stay the same, while the rates on their assets will increase, creating more profitability.

At the same time, you need to remember that interest rates don't always go up. Depending on the market and the federal government, rates might drop, sometimes quite low. If that happens, the value of your mortgage REIT may be affected.

As you can see, the risks with mortgage REITs are a bit more complex than Equity REITs.

Here is a quick list of things to consider regarding mortgage REITs:

- Mortgage REITs borrow considerably more to fund their operations. They can borrow up to 85% of their market value of assets, while equity REITs typically stay in the 25%-50% range.
- The dividends have become more unpredictable over the years.
- Mortgage REITs are more vulnerable to interest rate fluctuations.

Hybrid REITs

With such a cool name, you may be drawn to a hybrid REIT. How are they different from equity and mortgage REITs, and why might they be best for you?

The truth is that they don't differ much from those two but rather combine them, adding the benefits - and, yes, some of the downsides - of both to your portfolio. Unsurprisingly, a hybrid REIT combines equity and mortgage REITs. By diversifying across these particular types of trusts, hybrids can get the benefits of both but with less risk.

If you are an investor who is still determining what type of REIT is right for you, then a hybrid might be a good option. A hybrid REIT can give someone peace of mind knowing they are essentially getting the best of both worlds by removing the worry of making the right or wrong choices.

Another benefit of a hybrid REIT is that it allows the management team to pick and choose investments based on the market, industry, and other factors. They can decide that perhaps now isn't the time to put faith into more real estate being bought and developed, and they want to focus more of the trust on existing mortgages instead. On the other hand, maybe they think the economy favors people and businesses buying locations and property. If that is the case, they can focus the trust more on the equity side to benefit from that.

The versatility provided by a hybrid REIT is one of the main reasons people are drawn to them. They can change and fluctuate, but typically, this type of trust is weighted to one side more than the other: they are either more into the equity or mortgage side.

Your portfolio and investing plan will determine if you invest in a hybrid REIT. Having a single REIT that can make both equity and mortgage investments intrigues some investors; it feels like having the best of both worlds. Of course, the drawback is that the weighting of the trust can shift, giving you less influence over the placement in your portfolio. You are giving up more power to the people running your trust. Yet, that shouldn't necessarily be a bad thing, right? If you trust them with your money, you should trust them with their decisions. However, if you want to have much more say in where your money goes and the selection process, you should avoid them. You are giving the trust's management team more power with a hybrid REIT. That might be fine for some people but a sticking point for others.

You will have more influence over the makeup of your

portfolio if you choose equity or mortgage REITs since there will be an unwavering sectoral concentration.

OTHER TYPES OF REITS

Within each broader REIT type, niche REITs exist that can focus on particular businesses or even entire industries. Here are just some of the many niche REITs.

Healthcare REITs: As you would expect, healthcare REITs relate to property in the healthcare field. Places like hospitals, senior living facilities, doctor's offices, and even science facilities are some property types found in this type of REIT.

Office REITs: Nearly every company needs an office somewhere. Even restaurants and retail businesses usually have an office or headquarters. Office REITs invest in these sorts of locations. From office parks to commercial spaces, these REITs have locations nationwide. They can be single-story buildings or vast complexes.

Residential REITs: This is one of the most popular types of REITs. A lot of residential REITs focus on apartment complexes, some focus on single-family houses, while others have a mix. They are found in almost every city in the country, in all types of neighborhoods. Over the last few years, the importance and popularity of apartment buildings have grown, and residential REITs have benefited from that, making them all the more attractive to investors. As long as the world's population keeps growing, residential REITs will always be a popular choice.

• • •

Retail REITs: From malls to shopping centers and individual brick-and-mortar stores, retail REITs focus on businesses of all types. They are very enticing to investors because of just how ubiquitous they are. Of course, they can be significantly affected by the economy. Retail REITs are sometimes the first to get hit when the economy is suffering, or a recession is present. But when the economy is good, they're at the top of the heap.

Timberland REITs: Many people don't think about natural resources when considering REITs, but as long as society is moving forward, timber is needed. That is why some people specifically seek out timberland REITs. This type of trust invests in and manages various types of real estate used for its trees, which are harvested to produce several everyday, common, and essential products. Again, as long as the population keeps growing, timberland REITs will always be an attractive choice.

Infrastructure REITs: As technology advances, infrastructure REITs will be even more popular. This type of trust focuses on property or land used to establish cell phone towers, fiber optics, or other infrastructure-related buildings. While there aren't as many of these locations, it is essential to remember that they sell for a high price and are long-term investments. In other words, when a company buys land to build a tower or infrastructure project, they will likely be there - and paying out - for a long time. At the rate technology is progressing, these REITs are only going to grow in number.

• • •

Industrial REITs: If you have ever seen a warehouse or industrial building, such as a factory or distribution center, you know the type of property associated with industrial REITs. These buildings and properties are often long-term investments that can stand for decades or even centuries. That may be something to consider if you want to create generational wealth.

Hospitality REITs: Hotels, motels, and restaurants will always be needed. While their popularity and profit can sometimes wax or wane, they will forever be around. Hospitality REITs are related to this industry and these specific businesses.

Specialty REITs: Can't choose which one is right for you? Do you want a mix of everything? A specialty REIT might be right for you. From county prisons to schools, farmland, and more, specialty REITs don't have just one type of property they invest in. For that reason alone, they are attractive to many.

THE RIGHT REIT FOR YOU

So now you have learned a lot - a whole lot - about REITs, how they work, what they specialize in, and their pros and cons. Let's say you're entirely on board with buying into a REIT. That is all well and good, but how do you find the one that is right for you? It goes beyond just deciding that you want to become a shareholder for a REIT related to retail, apartments, or industrial locations. You must consider other things to ensure you pick the perfect one unique to your wants and needs.

Management

You always need to remember that with REITs, you are not just buying into an idea or industry; you are buying into a team that will work on your behalf. Be aware that you're not picking and choosing the properties you are putting your cash into. You are instead placing your money - and your trust - in a team of trained professionals who understand the market, know the risks and benefits, and can help you turn a profit by managing the trust.

It is always best to have total faith in the management team you are giving your hard earned money to. Kick the tires, look under the hood, and understand their view of the market, opinions, and goals. Make sure they have a track record you believe in and that it aligns with your goals and what you want to achieve by investing. Remember, you are basically hiring these people to handle your money. You should trust them above everything else, right?

When studying a management team while making your REIT choices, you should consider how they are compensated. This varies from one management team to another. If the team you are looking into is compensated based on their performance, they will probably work even harder to make sure your investment turns a profit. That is because the better your REIT does, the better they do. They are putting their necks on the line.

I'll review things to look at when analyzing a REIT's management team later in the book.

Diversification

The real estate market might be slow to move at times, but it is majorly consequential when it does. In other words, it feels incredible when the good times are here! But when times are bad, it really hurts. Therefore, you are putting yourself at serious risk if you aren't diversifying your investment smartly.

If you select niche REITs to capitalize on particular industries or markets, you must pay closer attention to your portfolio. Since niche REITs focus on specific sectors, they may be more volatile than REITs that invest in many sectors or industries. Whichever approach you take, ensure you are diversified. Again, I'll talk more about diversification later on.

Consider Your Own Financial Goals

What do you want to achieve? How much portfolio growth do you want to see? Is there a certain amount of income you want to generate? How involved do you want to be? Are you investing in a REIT simply to make money or to affect and be a part of a specific industry? Do you want to assemble a portfolio of niche REITs or invest in a single REIT that diversifies for you? All of this should be taken into consideration when making your choice.

You now have a better idea of what awaits you and which REITs could be suitable for you, but you need to consider the specifics of each type when choosing a REIT - and the management team - that will help you achieve a healthy financial future.

Once you have decided which REIT type you want to invest in - Equity, Mortgage, or Hybrid - it is time to create a strategy for investing. The next chapter will give you all the information you need to get started with an easy-to-follow, no-BS blueprint.

CHAPTER 3
THE NO-BS BLUEPRINT FOR REIT INVESTING

"Don't make the process harder than it is."

JACK WELCH

Here is something that many real estate experts won't tell you about REITs: they're pretty simple. That's right; they are not that complicated. Even though you have already learned a lot about them, the bottom line is and always will be this: REITs are investment trusts tied to specific types of real estate. That's all you truly need to know.

Sadly, many experts, analysts, and investors will try to complicate things for you and make the entire process of finding the right REIT way more confusing than it needs to be. If they make the process complex, you are more likely to have them do the leg work for you and give them a cut. But that won't happen here. Instead, I have an easy-to-follow blueprint to quickly connect you with the right REIT.

STEP 1: FIGURE OUT WHAT YOU WANT

Before you can *get* what you want, you have to know *what* you want. This is true for everything from dinner to REITs.

To know what you want and how to get there, break it down the "SMART" way. SMART stands for Specific, Measurable, Attainable, Relevant, and Timely. Following this path will help lay a foundation and give you clarity.

First, make your goal Specific. Are you trying to make money for retirement? Are you attempting to build up enough cash for a down payment on a house? Do you need a new car? What is your goal when you are finding a REIT? This is the first and most important thing you should address before you move on and start the selection process.

As for Measurable, that means that you need to be able to monitor and track how well your investment is doing. Are you getting close to your goal? Do you need to change things? Progress is measurable and necessary when it comes to investing. Don't mindlessly put your money into a REIT and hope for the best. You should keep tabs on how well things are going and make adjustments based on that.

Attainable goals are vital. This is a crucial part of your blueprint and plans moving forward. Is the goal you've set for yourself realistic? Can you truly attain it? Is the age you want to retire achievable? You need to be honest with yourself and create a set of goals you can reach. Now, that isn't to say you shouldn't stretch yourself and reach high, but if you want to make a million dollars in one year, that probably isn't going to happen.

And what is Relevant? Think of it in terms of a relevant strategy for you. Your goals should be relevant to you and your daily life. Why is this so important? Well, this will give you the drive to do better and treat your investments seriously. It will also help keep you on track whenever things take an unwanted turn. In investing, the road can get rocky, and the market can sometimes be unkind to you. But if you are fighting for a goal relevant to you and possibly your family (a new house, an incredible vacation to Italy you've always dreamed of, your daughter's college funds), then you will be able to stick with it through good times and bad. It will mean more to you if the goals you are working toward are relevant to your life and the well-being of those you love.

And, of course, there is the last part of your SMART goal. Being Timely means being on a schedule. Do you want to achieve a particular financial goal by the end of the month? The end of the quarter? The end of the year? In other words, it means holding yourself accountable and creating a plan that can achieve your goal by a particular time frame. A deadline will keep you on track. "By June 30th, my investment will make X amount of dollars" is the sort of timely goal many people subscribe to. If they don't achieve that goal, they must decide whether to change their investment strategy.

Being honest and accountable is extremely important here. If you don't create a solid goal, you won't have anything to aim for and you'll never know if you're on the right track.

STEP 2: DETERMINE YOUR BUDGET

Knowing how much you are willing to invest will play a significant role in shaping and achieving your financial goals. You will need to look at your finances and determine how much you are ready to set aside for your investments. Compare how much you have and how much you can comfortably commit. Be honest with yourself about how well you are doing financially. If you are married or have a family, discuss it with your spouse so you are on the same page. A good rule when starting is to be conservative. You don't want to bet the family farm on a REIT, even if it seems like the best investing opportunity you have ever seen.

People follow multiple types of budgeting strategies when they are putting together their investing plans. Some are rather aggressive; they want to go big right away and will invest all of their available cash at the beginning of their journey. While this can sometimes pay off because, frankly, the more you risk, the more you stand to make, it can also be your downfall since price fluctuations will have a bigger impact on your investment. When you are following an aggressive budget strategy, you might run out of money sooner than you think.

Others will be more moderate with their budget. They follow the slow and steady approach and have a precise schedule they set for themselves without deviating from it. At the same time, they will not be too cautious. They will commit to a decent amount of money to invest right at the beginning, but they will pace out their investments over time. The concept of pacing your investments over time is often called Dollar Cost Averaging (DCA). It's when you invest a set amount of money each month over a long period of time instead of dumping all of your cash into the market at once. Doing this will result in more stable investments and help avoid massive portfolio fluctuations when the markets experience more volatility.

And then there are those who are very conservative. They have a set amount to invest and won't put in a penny more. They will also sometimes pull their money out when the market isn't favorable to them or they don't feel comfortable about how things are going, which isn't necessarily good. If you pull your money out when the market isn't favorable and put it back in when it's doing well, you will eventually erode your capital. One of the best times to invest is when the market isn't doing well, so your investments hit a growth spurt when the market turns around!

So, how do you determine a budget that works for you? A great place to start is by using an online budget calculator. Keep in mind you will need all your income and expense figures handy, and make sure to enter all the numbers correctly. It might take some time to plug everything in, but it's much faster than doing it by hand and worth it, in the long run, to know exactly what you're working with.

After you run the numbers, if you still aren't sure how much to invest, 5% to 15% of your income is an excellent place to start. Go with 5% for conservative, 10% for modest, or 15% for aggressive.

One thing to remember is that investing in REITs is a long-term game. Once the money has been invested, it needs to stay there to make you a profit and generate a healthy income. The longer you keep your money invested, the more you'll make, generally speaking. You need to be comfortable not accessing your investment capital. Think about this before you choose the amount you are investing.

Tip: If you are already contributing to an investment portfolio, determine how much of your monthly contributions you want to shift to REITs. For example, if you are already contributing 10% of your income, consider putting 3% of that towards REITs. It is completely up to you!

STEP 3: RESEARCH

As you read previously, picking the right REIT involves some research, including looking at the management team; what is their success rate? What are their goals? How are they compensated? Evaluate what matters most to you. Also think about the type of industry or property that you believe has the most promise and the best chance to help you achieve your financial goals.

Remember, you're not just choosing a REIT because the numbers look good now. You need to go through a process of screening and consideration. This will be expanded on later in the book.

STEP 4: EVALUATE AND SCORE

A plan is only as good as its results. That is why the last part of the process is to evaluate and score your strategy to see how well it could perform.

How do you evaluate a REIT and determine if it's a good investment? You have a few ways to choose from. Firstly, there is the Net Asset Value (NAV), which will calculate a REITs value by assessing the fair market value of real estate assets minus liabilities. NAV is useful in determining if the share price is considered high, low, or just right. I'll expand more on this concept later.

There are also other financial metrics you can look at to determine the value of a REIT and estimate where it could go against its current price. In the chapters ahead, I will give you a simple system to help you evaluate a REIT in less than 30 minutes and determine if it's right for you.

Anytime you invest, you must ensure it's worth your hard-earned money. You need to shortlist the REITs you're considering investing in, then look at the numbers. Looking at the numbers means analyzing the REITs. Keep in mind that analyzing REITs is similar to other stocks, so if you already have experience looking at and scoring stocks, you are ahead of the game. If you don't have any prior experience in this realm, that's ok! I'll teach you everything you need to know.

One thing to note is that traditional metrics like price-to-earnings ratio and earnings-per-share are unreliable when it comes to REITs. What metrics do you use, then? A standard REIT metric mentioned previously is the Net Asset Value. If the NAV isn't available online, you may need to do some calculations yourself. This approach to market value is much more accurate. Again, we'll look at NAV in more detail later in the book.

Another common method is the top-down and bottom-up analysis. The top-down perspective shows that REITs can be affected by all things that affect supply and demand. Interest rates have an effect, but so do population and job growth. Bottom-up, on the other hand, focuses on the company that owns the REIT specifically. This viewpoint is that each REIT is different and needs to be analyzed based on the company that runs it.

Now that you have a basic understanding of how to put together a plan that works for you, here is something important to remember: if you want to make a change, you can. If your goals have changed, which they most likely will at some point in your life, create a new plan. You will not get far in any investment if you aren't following a plan that works for you.

Moving on, it is time we determine how you will sift through the myriad of existing REITs. Now more than ever, there are so many options regarding the type of REIT you can put your money into, and you can waste a lot of time not knowing how to find the best ones for you. Thankfully, you are about to learn a method that will save you hours, if not days, of analysis.

CHAPTER 4
SCREENING AND EVALUATING REITS

"The quality of your life is built on the quality of your decisions."

WESAM FAWZI

Making the right choice about anything - from the food you eat to the places you live to the people you associate with - is about screening and evaluating your options. Making the right selection for you will help you achieve your goals and live the life you desire.

The same applies when it comes to finding the right REIT. You will have to go through a precise, personal, and honest process that will allow you to arrive at your final destination: a REIT that can help you achieve your financial goals.

Some people believe the right REIT is simply the one that will perform well in the current market and give you a short-term windfall. Not true. Instead, the best REIT is the one that will provide you with long-term growth, stable income and make it through the inevitable economic storms. The right REIT should perform well and produce for you through good times and bad.

But how do you find that mythical REIT? What are the best tools to dig deeper, kick the tires, look under the hood, and determine if a particular REIT is right for you? You were promised a 6-step process to help you do that, so here it is!

WHAT TO LOOK FOR WHEN FILTERING THROUGH REITS

First and foremost, if you are a new investor, it would be wise to avoid putting your money into a mortgage REIT. We looked at this type of REIT before, and while it comes with many benefits, additional risk and complexity is involved. Instead, it is wise to focus on equity or hybrid REITs when starting.

The following financial metrics are what you will use as a part of your 6-step screening and evaluation process. You'll need to use an online screener as part of this process, which will help narrow in on the ideal REIT for you. Many screeners are available online, but a great one to start with is finviz.com. After we review the financial metrics, I'll provide an overview of how to use the screener.

Before we dive in, I want to mention that this is the book's most technical chapter, so take your time. Go at your own pace, and don't jump ahead. What you learn in the paragraphs to come will set the foundation for your REIT investing journey. The foundation you build now will determine your future success, so make sure it's solid.

STEP 1: DIVIDEND YIELD

Whether you're a beginner or a seasoned investor, you need to know a thing or two about a "dividend yield." This is a crucial metric as it's one of the main reasons people invest in REITs. The dividend yield is how you will generate income through real estate without owning physical property.

A dividend yield - sometimes called a percentage - is a financial ratio (dividend over price) that showcases how much a company, or REIT in our case, pays out in dividends each year relative to its price on the market. In other words, a dividend yield indicates how much income an investor can earn.

Dividend Yield = Annual Dividends Paid Per Share/Price Per Share

So, if a particular stock pays a quarterly dividend of 75 cents per share, the annual dividend is $3 per share (4 quarters per year, therefore, 75 cents multiplied by 4 equals $3). Let's say the stock trades at $125 per share. That would give you a dividend yield of 2.4%.

A good dividend yield for a REIT is generally between 2% and 6%. As you dive deeper into REITs, you'll see some that pay as high as 15% or even 20%, but be cautious when you see numbers like those. It may seem like a great opportunity at first glance, but long-term sustainability comes into question. When a yield hits 10% or higher, exercise caution.

A great example of long-term stability is a REIT called Realty Income Corp. Since 2003, it has paid an average dividend of around 5%. Some years were substantially higher, and some were lower, but 5% is the general range. As of this book's written date, it's also raised the dividend payout for 102 consecutive quarters. That's 25 years! Granted, all REITs won't have a track record like that, but it is an example of what to look for.

Now that you know the basics, consider your minimum acceptable yield. How much income are you looking for? What is your best-case and worst-case scenario? Consider how much you want to earn and determine how much you'll need to invest. For example, if you want to make $1000 a month from a REIT with a 5% annual dividend yield, you'll need to get your investment in that REIT to $240,000. If that seems like a significant investment for an income of $1000 a month, think again.

What kind of property can you get for $240,000 nowadays? In most major cities, you would be hard-pressed to find a house for that price. In some cities, that's just a down payment! But let's say you can buy a small house or condo where you live for that amount. Now think about how much you could rent it for and what you would have left over after paying the expenses of owning that property - mortgage payment, property taxes, utilities, maintenance, etc. You would be *lucky* to have a couple hundred dollars in monthly profit.

I really want to drive this point home because this step will help set the foundation for which REIT you choose.

I'll also talk about dividend reinvestment plans (DRIP) later, which will accelerate your results and help you reach your financial goals faster.

STEP 2: RETURN ON EQUITY (ROE)

Something to consider when you are choosing your REIT is a classic investing term called return on equity. In the simplest terms, this ratio calculates the return generated on the total equity invested in a property. As you can imagine, it is often used in real estate.

There is no specific number for ROE, but limiting your

selections to those in the top 50% of the group is an excellent place to start. This will allow you to choose from the best and healthiest REITs.

STEP 3: PRICE-TO-BOOK RATIO (P/B)

Price-to-book ratio is a tool investors use to compare a company's market capitalization to the book value, which is a great way to find undervalued companies. It is determined by dividing a company's current stock price by its book value per share. Think of it as comparing the cost of stock to its actual market value.

For REITs, a general guideline is to look for a price-to-book ratio of 1 or less. That means you are getting more value than you pay for. More bang for the buck, as it were. That said, it's ok if the ratio is slightly higher than 1, but don't let it go past 1.5. The closer the P/B gets to 2, the more overvalued the REIT is and the higher the chance of a downward price correction. This is an essential factor when making your final REIT selection.

STEP 4: FUNDS-FROM-OPERATIONS (FFO) & EARNINGS-PER-SHARE (EPS)

Funds from operations is a measurement used to determine a company's operating performance; in our case, a REIT. The easiest way to think about it is it's a measure of the cash generated by a REIT. As for earnings-per-share, this value determines how much money a company makes for each share or stock. It looks at a company's overall total profit after its investments. FFO is typically more accurate for REITS, so I'll refer to it.

The number we're looking at for FFO is the payout ratio,

which is the percentage of FFO paid out as dividends. REITS have higher-than-average payouts, so a 70%-80% payout ratio is typical. However, a ratio close to 100%, or higher than 100%, can signal wavering financial performance and often means a dividend cut could happen soon.

A general guideline for FFO payout ratios is as follows:

- 35%-60% is considered the safest
- 60%-80% is moderately safe
- Over 80% is risky

Remember, the closer to 100%, the higher the risk.

Tip: If you cannot determine where the payout ratio is coming from on your screener (FFO or EPS), that's ok. Set it up and move on.

STEP 5: DEBT-TO-EQUITY (D/E) RATIO

Any company you invest in should be carrying a manageable amount of debt. Why is this so important? If a company, or REIT in our case, is carrying too much debt, that shows it isn't handling its business well. It gives you insight into the management team running the REIT.

How much debt is too much debt? Luckily, the debt-to-equity ratio is a way to determine just that. It's calculated by dividing the debt by the shareholders' equity. For example, if a company is $200,000 in debt and has $100,000 in shareholder equity, that would equal a D/E ratio of 2.

Try to stick with REITs with a D/E ratio of two or less. Generally speaking, a D/E ratio of two or less indicates a company with a healthy amount of debt.

While you can use countless other metrics, the five we just

reviewed - Dividend Yield, Return-on-Equity, Price-to-Book ratio, Funds-from-Operations, and Debt-to-Equity - should form the core of your screening process. Ideally, the REIT(s) you invest in will meet all five screening metrics. Once you apply these metrics to your screener, you will have an excellent list of REITs to choose from!

HOW TO USE A SCREENER

Before we move on to step 6, I want to teach you how to use an online stock screener. It's time to implement what you have learned and create a list of potential REITs to invest in!

Here is a checklist that summarizes the screening and evaluation criteria you just learned:

1) Dividend Yield: Determine your acceptable yield. Anything up to 6% is considered good and sustainable.

2) Return on Equity: Top 50% of the group is best.

3) Price-to-Book Ratio: less than 1.

4) FFO Payout Ratio: 70%-80% is common. General guideline; 35%-60% safest, 60%-80% moderately safe, over 80% starts getting risky.

5) Debt-to-Equity Ratio: 2 or less.

The following steps will guide you through using the finviz.com screener. Again, you can try out multiple screeners and use the one you like best.

1) Go to finviz.com and click on the "Screener" tab.

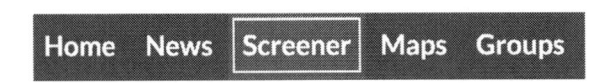

| Home | News | Screener | Maps | Groups |

2) Click on the "Custom" tab below the screening criteria. This tab will allow you to add the screening criteria you just

read about to the list of REITs you'll soon create. Next, make sure the "Settings" button in the top right hand corner is selected and select the following options: P/B, Return on Equity, Dividend Yield, Payout Ratio, Total Debt/Equity. You should now see a column for each selection at the top of the stock list, and you can click on each column heading to sort them by ascending or descending order.

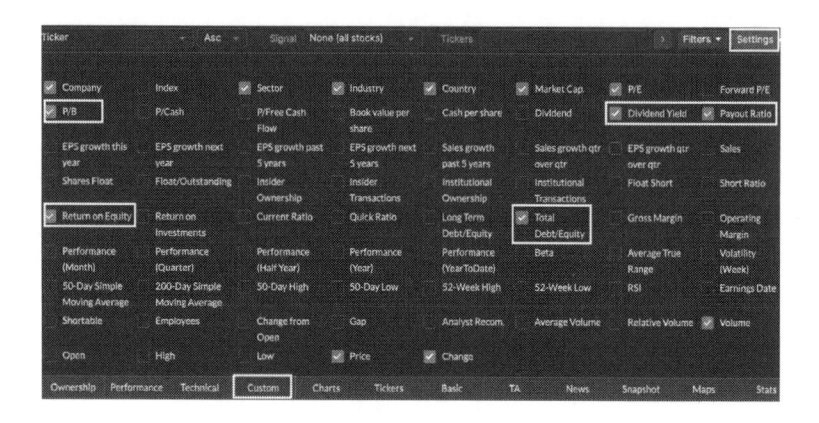

3) Click on "Filters" near the top right part of the screen, which will open the screening selections. Next, click on the "All" tab to display all of the filtering options. Change the "Sector" option to "Real Estate" to only include REITs in your list. Otherwise, you will have stocks from every industry in your screening list. Now update the following options based on the screening criteria you learned: Dividend Yield, P/B, Payout Ratio, Return on Equity, and Debt/Equity.

GETTING RICH WITH REIT INVESTING 41

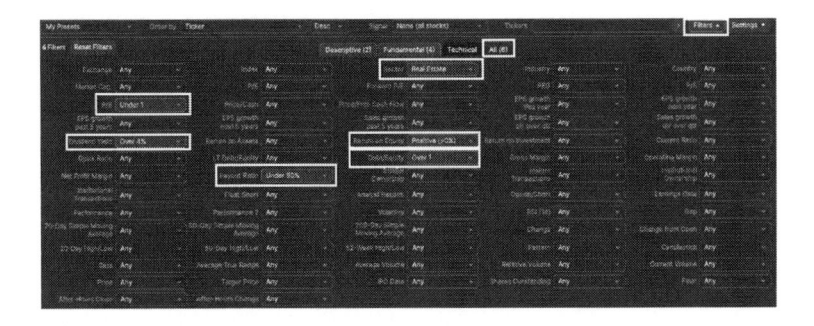

[screener interface image]

And voila! You now have a filtered REIT list based on your screening criteria.

Keep in mind the criteria suggestions for each metric are on the conservative side. If you want to adjust the numbers and create screening criteria based on your own ideas, feel free to do so. Remember the example of Realty Income Corp? It's one of the market's most stable and well-performing REITs, and its P/B ratio at the time of this writing is 1.37. That shows there is wiggle room in these metrics. Experiment and make them your own. Or, if you want to stay as conservative as possible, stick to the suggested guidelines.

Tip: If the list of REITs you see is too short - or if you aren't seeing any at all - you might need to adjust your screening metrics, as they may be too conservative for the current market environment.

Now that you have the first 5 steps locked in, it's time for the last step in your screening and evaluating process.

STEP 6: HOW TO ANALYZE A REIT'S MANAGEMENT TEAM

Have you ever gotten a bad feeling about someone but don't know why? You can't put your finger on it, but you feel uneasy around them. This is your intuition warning you about someone for one or several reasons. The same can happen when looking at a REIT's management team. They are human, after all. You might not be sure why you feel uneasy about them, but you get the heebie-jeebies.

While having actual numbers and statistics to look at when making your decision is essential, it is vital to remember that you should look at certain things beyond numbers and figures when reviewing a REIT's management team. They might be putting forward fantastic financial milestones and achievements, but you need to look deeper than that. Why? Well, maybe they are new to the industry and had dumb luck on their side. Perhaps they just happened to put their shareholder's money in the right market at the right time, and no skill led them to success. And maybe that luck is going to run out. What happens when the real estate market hits a rough patch, and all REITs suffer? Is this a team that can get through the turbulent times?

Think of a REIT's management team as a ship on the high seas. A vessel pushing through the ocean might be beautiful and expertly made, but if it's filled with a captain and crew who don't know what they are doing, it will undoubtedly crash upon the rocky shores of an island. In other words, it takes the right people to ensure the ship arrives at its destination. It takes the right people to ensure the money you invest in a REIT is used wisely. Here are some ways to tell you are putting your money, time, and belief into a team that will treat your money right.

. . .

Over-Optimism

To start with, you should be wary of any overly optimistic team. You may encounter this when you are on the hunt for your REIT.

Over-optimism is usually because a management team is desperate for investors. Consider this a red flag. You never want to invest in a team desperate for business since that's usually a sign they don't know what they're doing.

As stated before, no market is free of risk. All markets will have ups and downs, good times and bad. That is the nature of investing. Nothing is immune, whether it be REITs, cryptocurrency, the stock market, or foreign exchange. If you find a REIT management team who says they have the silver bullet to avoid any downturns in the market, you are being lied to.

Now, optimism isn't all bad. They can believe in themselves and their ability to overcome tough times that will inevitably come, but they should be realistic above all else. They should be honest and admit they can't avoid all downturns, but they should also give reasons why they believe they can get you and your investment through it. There is a difference between confidence and hubris.

Past Decisions

Generally speaking, you know how well a company will work in the future by looking at the choices they have made in the past.

You need to look at the track record of a REIT management team. That means you need to know the property acquisitions they have made; REITs are all about real estate, after all. While buying into a REIT is quite different from purchasing a piece of property, there is something to consider when looking at past acquisitions made by a company. You see how well they know the market. You are also seeing how well a company can make sizable, long-term investments or how well they can turn a property around and make a profit on a piece of real estate.

This will let you know how well the team handles the market and what they consider when investing in real estate. If you don't like the decisions they made with past acquisitions, you can be sure you won't like future ones either.

Common Interests

Whether making new friends or starting to date someone, you need to share some common interests. You will not get far with them if you don't see eye-to-eye on some crucial things, which is also true for a REIT management team.

You need to know they hold the same values you do. Are they looking to make a massive splash on the market and make tons of money quickly, involving significant risk? Or are they trying to make sizable, consistent returns over time? Which of those relates to you more? You don't want a team trying to make a massive windfall on the market as soon as possible, especially if that involves significant risk. At the same time, you also don't want a team that will work *too* slowly. The team needs to be in a goldilocks zone where they take calculated risks based on their experience.

Finding the sweet spot of a consistently well-performing REIT with a solid management team is the combination you want. Remember, any management team should always have your interests as the shareholder in mind.

CHOOSING YOUR REIT

You have now gone through the 6-step screening and evaluation process and are ready to select your REIT! Think of the first five steps as the first date; you are getting to know someone. The sixth step is going past that first date and getting to know their values and personality.

Here are all six screening and evaluation steps together:
1) Dividend Yield
2) Return on Equity
3) Price-to-Book Ratio
4) FFO Payout Ratio
5) Debt-to-Equity Ratio
6) Evaluate the REIT management team

These steps lay the foundation for generating wealth from real estate without owning a single physical property. I recommend returning to this section regularly and re-reading it until you know it like the back of your hand.

INVESTING IN YOUR REIT

You've decided which REIT you want to invest in; now what? There are different investing methods, but one mentioned earlier in the book stands out above all the rest; dollar-cost averaging (DCA).

Dollar-cost averaging is simple and effective. You invest on a schedule with a predetermined amount of money, no matter the current share price. That's it. For example, invest $100 on the 15th of each month or $50 every two weeks. Whatever the frequency and dollar amount is, the key is consistency; that is what makes dollar-cost averaging so effective. Because you're buying shares at different price points over long periods, you reduce the volatility of your investment and lower your average cost per share.

Let's say you have $10,000 to invest and put the whole amount into a REIT in one shot. The value of your investment will fluctuate wildly with the ups and downs of the market because you bought $10,000 worth of shares at one price. Instead, imagine if you slowly invested it over a year or two at regular intervals, buying at different price points along the way; high, low, and everywhere in between. Your investment is now less impacted by the ups and downs of the market because your money is spread out across different price points. Consistency combined with a long-term investing mindset will generate wealth.

If you are unsure how much to invest, refer back to Section 2 in Chapter 3, which discusses determining your budget. As for how often, a good starting point is to invest a bit of money every time you get paid.

DIVIDEND REINVESTMENT PLAN (DRIP)

Dividend reinvestment plans are one of the easiest ways to accelerate your investing goals. When a REIT pays a dividend, you usually receive it as cash in your brokerage account. However, with a DRIP, the dividend automatically gets reinvested and buys you more stock! I'm sure you have heard the saying "Make your money work for you." That is precisely what a DRIP does.

Ensure the investing platform you use has DRIPs available to capitalize on them. Unless you are at the point where dividends are needed to supplement your income, set up a DRIP if it's available for your REIT.

If you don't have a brokerage account yet, I'll talk more about different brokerages you can start with later.

I know this chapter had a lot of information to take in. If you're new to investing - especially in REITs - your head might be spinning, but that is why I have broken down the process into easy-to-follow steps that will help you get from Point A to Point B, C, D, and beyond.

Come back to this chapter as many times as needed. It's the foundation for your REIT investing journey, and understanding every detail is critical. If you don't perform the due diligence and do the work, you won't get the results you desire.

Now you know how to size up a REIT and create a list of investment opportunities. But before you invest your heard-earned money, there is something else to consider - how are REITs registered and how will that influence your investment decision? There are publicly-traded, non-traded, and private REITs. Each type will have distinct pros and cons, so let's dive in and discover which type is right for you.

CHAPTER 5
INVESTING IN PUBLICLY TRADED REITS

"Know what you own, and know why you own it."

PETER LYNCH

What is a publicly traded REIT, what does it add to your portfolio, and why might it be right for you?

Remember how we have said there is no sure thing when it comes to investing? That is still true, but you are entitled to a bit less risk when investing in publicly traded REITs. That is because, like stocks on Wall Street and beyond, publicly-traded REITs operate within a system that has rules, which keeps the business in check, giving you more security and stability. If you understand how stocks trade on the market, then you know how publicly-traded REITs work! They have their stocks listed for trading on an exchange like the NYSE or NASDAQ, have their securities registered with the SEC, and submit regular reports to the SEC. As you can see, this provides a lot of checks and balances and ensures that specific rules must be followed at all times.

Another advantage to publicly-traded REITs is that they are generally liquid investments, making them easy to buy and sell just like any other stock listed on an exchange. The public can also easily access real-time market pricing for publicly listed REIT shares. For these reasons, I always recommend investing in publicly-traded REITs.

That said, there are non-traded REITs whose stocks are registered with the SEC and submit routine reports to the SEC, but are not listed on an exchange and traded in the open market. We'll look at those a bit later.

Note: The list of REITs you created in your stock screener are all publicly-traded REITs.

With the multitude of publicly-traded REITs available, there are also REIT ETFs. ETF stands for Exchange-Traded Fund. Most newcomers don't know about this unique, one-of-a-kind investment. Even those who have years of investing under their belt may not know much about them. I'll discuss ETFs in more detail later.

PROS & CONS

What are some pros and cons of investing in a publicly traded REIT? There are quite a few, and you must be well-informed before investing.

THE PROS

Easy Investing

One thing holding people back from investing in REITs is that they feel it will take a lot of work. They think there is so much to learn, so many variables to keep track of, and so many ways to get bogged down, slowed down, or confused. Not so!

As you just read, investing in publicly-traded REITs couldn't be easier. The ease of investing is perhaps the biggest reason you should consider putting your money into publicly-traded REITs. Buying one is just like buying stock in Amazon, Apple, or any other publicly traded company.

Size

Some investors feel more comfortable putting their money into a large project with many other investors. It makes it feel like the risk is spread thinly across everyone involved. Investing in a publicly traded REIT is a way to invest in a large-scale project with a lot of people and money. It is the epitome of big.

Income

You can earn significant income from publicly-traded REITs if you play your cards right. REITs tend to pay higher dividends than the average stock, and since there are many REITs to choose from, finding one that meets your dividend yield criteria will be easy. And remember the concept of DRIPs (dividend reinvestment plans)? They will supercharge your earnings!

. . .

You Can Be Part Of Big Deals

When investing in real estate, some people want to put their cash into malls, apartment buildings, shopping centers, and more. But, sadly, you might not always have the sort of money to invest in those property types.

Publicly-traded REITs, however, allow you to put your money into that type of real estate. By investing in a publicly traded REIT, you are a part of the real estate deals that are often off-limits for most of the population. This is another example of how powerful REITs can be.

Protection

The SEC is a vital governmental body overseeing all the moves in any market. They are the watchdogs who tend to any problems and lawbreaking related to the stock market, and they also have an eye on publicly traded REITs. They can ensure that all players follow the rules, treat their investors fairly, and adhere to the government's regulations.

If you are looking for an extra layer of security, that is the SEC. But you can only gain access to the oversight of the SEC if you are investing in publicly traded REITs.

As you can see, there are many pros. But what about the cons? Like with anything, there are a few to be aware of.

THE CONS

Volatility

When people talk about investing, ideally, they want to put their money in a market to make it grow. It makes perfect sense and is why so many people have made millions in various markets throughout the last few generations.

If you've ever seen a graph or chart showcasing the stock market's history (S&P 500, for example), there are sharp spikes that go up and down, indicating the value of the market. These ebbs and flows are typical, though they are usually not very drastic.

However, there have been times when the market *has* experienced a massive drop-off or gain. The large gains are celebrated, of course, but the significant drops cause serious concern. They are terrifying events for investors and the entire country because you're seeing your investment value sharply drop, and a weakened stock market can lead to a weakened economy. However, you only sometimes see significant highs and lows like that. Most of the time, the ups and downs are modest, and the market consistently rises over time. That is why so many people invest. These participants find stocks or REITs to believe in and watch their investments grow.

By putting your money into publicly-traded REITs, you are opening yourself up to the volatility that strikes the broader market occasionally. This will sometimes cause your investment to drop, but it will inevitably rebound and reach new highs. Some investors pull their money out at the first sign of volatility, but that is the last thing you should do. Instead, you must stick with it and keep your emotions out of it. Understand that the ebbs and flows of the market come with the territory, and you need to be smart about it. Don't jump at the first sign of trouble. It might sometimes feel uncomfortable, but it will keep your portfolio strong in the long run. No market is forever stable; that is the price of investing in an open market.

Fees

One of the biggest cons of investing in an open market is the number of fees that come with it. You can pay fees for buying a REIT, selling it, holding it, etc. It sometimes feels like you can't make a move without putting up more money somehow.

Publicly-traded REITs come with their own fees, some out in the open and some harder to find. Be aware of this when you are buying or selling REITs. Again, it cannot be avoided. It comes with the territory. I'll talk more about fees later.

Tangible Assets

Some people like to see - or hold - the things they buy. They want to get a good look at them, make sure they are real, and admire what they achieved.

When you invest in a publicly-traded REIT, you will likely never see the property you invested your money into. Sure, you'll know they exist, but you will most likely never walk up to the building you invested in. You just have to assume it's out there somewhere.

This is only a psychological con for investors, but it is legitimate, and it has led some people to hold back on investing in publicly traded REITs. They like to look at the things they invest in and help build. They may, however, miss out on some extraordinary investment opportunities.

HOW TO INVEST IN PUBLICLY TRADED REITS

Okay, so you've decided the pros outweigh the cons and want to invest in publicly-traded REITs. How do you actually do that? Well, the good news is that you've already done most of the work. You have read the previous chapters and know which one(s) you want to invest in. All that's left to do is open a brokerage account. Or, if you already have one, buy the REIT!

Due to the size of the dividends REITs provide, it may be wise to hold them in a tax-advantaged account, such as an

IRA, to delay paying taxes on the distribution. In Canada, this type of account is called a TFSA. In the UK, it's an ISA.

You have absorbed a lot of information up to this point, so let's break down the process a bit more to give you a refresher and as a way to provide you with even more details to set you up for success.

Open Your Brokerage Account

If you don't already have a brokerage account, it's time to get one. REITs, ETFs, stocks, bonds, and other types of assets may all be purchased and sold via a brokerage account.

There are several brokerages to pick from, and many of them provide fantastic low-cost options, including no minimum balance to start or maintain an account, no or low trading fees, and no monthly account fee. Before registering, it's crucial that you compare the various platforms. If your brokerage account doesn't need a minimum balance to open, you can deposit as little as a few hundred dollars and begin investing immediately.

Some examples of popular, user-friendly brokerages are Wealth Simple, E-Trade, and Robinhood. You can access them on your computer or an app on your phone. They are very user-friendly and have low fees. Funding your brokerage account is also incredibly easy; it's as simple as inputting your bank account number and sending the money to your brokerage!

As with everything, do your due diligence and research brokerages before opening an account to ensure you pick the one that suits you best.

Choose Your Industry

Whether you are a new or seasoned investor, you need to

take the time to determine which sector or industry you want to invest your money into. Each real estate sector has upwards of 200 publicly-traded REITs, making it difficult to decide which one to invest in. That's a good problem to have!

Do you want to put your cash into office buildings? Retail properties? Hotels? Residential? Hospitals? Communication centers? Data centers? Or do you want to buy a REIT that holds property in several industries? It is essential to take the time to figure out what you want *before* you invest.

Remember, because REITs invest in real estate, other variables besides market volatility can affect performance. Therefore investors must familiarize themselves with the threats and possibilities in the relevant sectors. This is your homework. Remember to do it, or it will bite you in the long run.

And, of course, before buying any REIT, you want to screen and evaluate them, as discussed in Chapter 4.

Purchase Your Publicly Traded REIT

Now comes the fun part: buying your publicly-traded REIT. It is time to put your money where your mouth is and let your investment journey begin. Now you must purchase the required shares in the REIT you have chosen. The number of shares you buy will depend on how much money you have to invest, which you have already determined in Chapter 3.

Tip: It is always better to gradually expand your portfolio over time instead of investing heavily in one thing. Diversification will make the rough times in the market more bearable.

BEST PRACTICES

One of the biggest mistakes you can make when investing is trying to make money quickly. Remember, this isn't a get-rich-quick scheme. One of the main things you want to consider is taking a long-term approach. If you commit to a long-term investing mindset and choose your REITs wisely, your investment will prosper. Anything worth doing takes time.

There will be risks involved in every choice and transaction you make. It is silly to think that you are invulnerable to losses and that every choice you make will be brilliant. Taking a loss here and there is inevitable; it's the cost of doing business. However, with risk comes reward. You can't make an omelet without breaking a few eggs. When your first inevitable loss comes, remember you're in this for the long haul. Your long-term mindset will keep you steadfast in your plan and guide you to success.

Regulate Your Emotions

Remember to keep your emotions - good or bad - out of the decision-making process. If you succeed early in your investing journey, you might become addicted to making a profit and want more. That could cause you to rush the process and jump into other opportunities without doing your due diligence. Early success can distort your view of the world; it makes you feel more powerful than you are. All it takes to walk away empty-handed are a few bad choices. If you swing big too many times and miss, you will end up with an empty wallet. If you are met with significant success early on, that's great! But stick to your plan and stay consistent.

The same is true for negative emotions. If the market turns and starts going against you, you may get the urge to sell everything and take what you have left. Fight that urge.

You'll eventually have nothing left if you continuously sell your investments during a dip. You may also want to tighten your wallet during these times, but that means you would miss out on some of the best times to invest. Remember the concept of dollar cost averaging? It will keep you on a regular investing schedule, including buying during the low points, which means you'll get great returns when things turn around. If you're inconsistent with your investing, at best, you'll walk away with the same amount you came in with. At worst, you'll walk away with nothing. Ups and downs are part of investing, but you will make money over time. Consistency over time wins. Stick to your plan.

Make Your Move

Another mistake to avoid is moving with haste. No proper investor will tell you to make rash and fast decisions with money. But they will also tell you not to wait *too* long either. If you have found a REIT you believe in and it meets your evaluation criteria, make your move. You can go down countless rabbit holes with hours of research and be no better off than when you started. Analysis paralysis is real. When you have the green light, go for it.

Do Your Homework

Finally, at the risk of sounding like a broken record, you must do the work above all else. Going through your evaluation criteria and doing your due diligence is the foundation of investing. Someone who was once poor can become a king, and someone on top could end up on the bottom, all faster than you can imagine. A careless investor will almost always end up filled with regret.

If you are new to investing, you may be nervous or overwhelmed by the sheer amount of information coming at you. That's normal. Most people feel that way when starting something new. The key is to keep your end goal in mind and take one step at a time. Remember, a journey of 1000 miles begins with a single step.

As you have seen, there are many benefits to investing in publicly-traded REITs. They are easy to access, have regulatory oversight, and have endless variety. But what about REITs that aren't publicly traded? Are they worth investing in? They have an added layer of complexity but can be lucrative if you know how to navigate them.

CHAPTER 6
INVESTING IN NON-TRADED REITS

"We must become more comfortable with probability and uncertainty."

NATE SILVER

Publicly-traded REITs are like buying a house in a bustling city with an active market. It's easy to sell when you want to. Non-traded REITs, however, can be like buying a mansion in a smaller, slower-paced town. Your home is worth significant money, but you'll have a more challenging time selling it.

When it comes to non-traded REITs, there are two types: Private REITs and PNLRs (public non-listed REITs). Let's look at the differences between the two in detail.

PRIVATE REITS

As you may have assumed by the word "private," these REITs are not exchanged in a marketplace. They don't provide shares that may be purchased and sold on a public stock exchange. Investments are made through direct investor solicitation or private placements, and private REITs often have rigid holding specifications. There may be very little or no program in place for you to sell your interest for five or more years. And it's not unheard of for sales to be below the REIT's value if they do provide a redemption program.

Furthermore, it is only permissible for accredited investors to make investments in these REITs. That is an essential piece of the private REIT puzzle. To be recognized as an accredited investor, you must fulfill minimum net worth and/or income requirements. Private REITs frequently concentrate on attracting big, institutional investors like pension funds and businesses with sizable endowments.

Last but not least, private REITs are exempt from SEC registration requirements. They also don't submit financial records. Individual investors who lack the knowledge and resources to comprehend and assess the appropriateness of a private REIT are exposed to significant risk due to the lack of oversight and transparency.

As a result, private REITs are only sometimes available to average investors and are not the best fit even when they are.

PNLR (PUBLIC NON-LISTED REIT)

There are also public non-listed REITs. They are a hybrid between private and publicly-traded REITs. They do not trade on exchanges, but they are registered with the SEC. Like private REITs, since they are not listed on public exchanges, they have lower volatility than publicly-traded REITs and offer a purer play on real estate, which appeals to some people. However, they are not without their barriers. PNLRs often require you to be an accredited investor like private REITs, and even though they are registered with the SEC, transparency and liquidity are common issues.

A non-traded REIT usually gets investors to put their money into a "blind pool." Investors have a general idea of what the REIT wants to accomplish, but there is typically no stated investment goal, and you won't have details about how your funds will be used. The investors know a bit about the REIT and properties they are investing in, but don't know much more than that.

After investors contribute the money needed to purchase shares of the REIT, general partners will use the accumulated capital to invest in the real estate properties chosen. After that, the REIT portfolio will be managed much like any other type of REIT. Eventually, 90% of the income will be distributed to the investors. Then an exit strategy is created by either liquidating the REIT's assets or listing it on an exchange and converting it into a publicly-traded REIT. Selling shares in a PLNR before the exit strategy is often tricky due to redemption restrictions.

SIMILARITIES & DIFFERENCES

What are some similarities and differences between non-traded and publicly-traded REITs?

Thankfully, publicly-traded REITs and PLNRs are registered with the SEC, which adds some comfort to those putting their money on the line. They have to follow the same regulations and guidelines presented by the government. They also must meet the 90% distribution rule. That means that at least 90% of the taxable income must be returned to the shareholders who put their money into it. There are differences, though, which are very important to remember as you contemplate investing in a non-traded REIT.

The biggest difference is that being eligible to invest in a non-traded REIT is much harder than a publicly-traded one. With a publicly-traded REIT, all you need is a brokerage account and enough funds to buy a single share (in some cases, a fraction of a share). But with a non-traded REIT, you must qualify as an accredited investor. That might not sound hard, but it is. To earn this title, you must have a net worth of $1,000,000 or an annual income over $200,000 as an individual, or $300,000 with a spouse, for the past two years. As you can imagine, this severely limits the pool of people involved in non-traded REITs.

Transparency is another major difference. With a non-traded REIT, investors might not have access to the actual properties the REIT has invested in and may only be aware of the general type of investment they are making. There is a significant lack of clarity regarding how the funds are used, and investors are often left in the dark.

And if you want to get your money back prematurely, that isn't easy. Generally speaking, your options to get your money back are to wait for it to become a publicly traded REIT or until the REIT liquidates its holdings. However, you can sell your share(s) whenever you are ready with publicly-traded REITs, which is a huge advantage.

PROS & CONS

Now that you know more about non-traded REITS, maybe you think this is the right choice for you. Before you make that decision, let's look at the pros and cons of non-traded REITs before you commit to investing in one.

· · ·

The Pros

Firstly, the biggest pro to a non-traded REIT is that you have the potential for a higher return on your investment since you will have to invest more to be a part of this type of REIT. That alone creates the potential for higher returns.

And while some people might not be happy with how long you have to let your money sit in a non-traded REIT, this can be a good thing. The inability to pull your investment out on a whim means you stand to make more money by riding out the real estate market's fluctuations. Instead, You can focus on the REIT's long-term goals and avoid second-guessing yourself and wondering if you should take your money and run.

The Cons

The biggest con is less oversight from government bodies, which means more risk. Yes, a PNLR is overseen by the SEC, but not with the same intensity and scrutiny. You are more exposed with a non-traded REIT.

It's also a lot harder to be part of a non-traded REIT. You must have a significant amount of money to invest. Most of us are not millionaires, so this is a con that prevents people from being involved altogether. But having that money is necessary because the upfront fees you have to pay to be part of a non-traded REIT are high, which is another big con pushing people away from investing in this type of REIT.

Additionally, the income distribution is not always reliable. Publicly-traded REITs have more reliable dividend yields, which helps you create a more detailed investing plan.

And getting your investment back (if you can) from a non-traded REIT can be convoluted and lengthy. Low liquidity can be a significant con because you may not be able to get your money out if the long-term prospects shift and start to look bleak.

Lastly, the fees. Since the people investing in non-traded REITs are generally much wealthier, the fees are much higher too. In fact, some fees can be as high as 12% to 15% of the money you invest. The return would have to be substantial to make it worth the money lost in fees.

Okay, you now know the specifics of non-traded REITs and the pros and cons. So, let's say you are still interested in being a part of one. How do you make that happen? What is the process of investing in this particular type of REIT?

HOW TO INVEST IN A NON-TRADED REIT

First and foremost, you must ensure you meet the accredited investor requirements. This is one of the biggest reasons beginners should typically stick with publicly-traded REITs. If you meet the accredited investor requirements, then and only then can you consider investing in a non-traded REIT.

Second, you will need to find a financial advisor who can find an investment opportunity for you. Remember, non-traded REITs typically aren't advertised to the general public, so finding one to invest in will take a bit more leg work. And when it comes to an investment advisor, you want to make sure they are someone you can trust. Performing due diligence on them is just as important as analyzing the REIT. Also, remember that the financial advisor, or whoever is connecting you to the investment opportunity, will take a fee or commission.

Third, I recommend you perform heavy due diligence on the management team. Just because a REIT is non-traded and, therefore, potentially able to make more money doesn't mean it will. As with any REIT, you need to analyze the team managing it and understand its track record. After all, due to the lack of transparency with non-traded REITs, you won't know much about the REIT's goals, so the management team will heavily influence your decision.

If you go the private route, you will have to do much more work. This path may give you the best chance of a substantial financial windfall, but you will need to handle every detail of the screening and evaluation yourself that is quickly done with online screeners for publicly-traded REITs, and sometimes handled by experts and analysts with PNLRs. That means asking for as many financial statements and projections the management team is willing to give and using a good old-fashioned calculator to figure out the metrics.

There are fewer guard rails, rules, regulations, and more risks with this type of REIT. But with so many restrictions and so much work required to benefit from it, why would anyone choose to invest in a non-traded REIT? That is a valid question with a valid answer that goes back to the pros we discussed earlier.

The truth is that many people have made significant money via non-traded REITs. Yes, you must put more money into it and cannot easily pull your investment out. Non-traded REITs also come with hefty fees and less oversight from the federal governmental bodies that usually protect you, which means you are exposing yourself to more risk. But the return on investment can often be very high. Some consider these the "expert" REITs that only the most seasoned and successful professionals use. When someone knows the REIT market well and has found success, they come to non-traded REITs. It's an exclusive club, and the process requires much more time, effort, and money, but it can pay off substantially. You will be putting more on the line, but greater risks might come with greater rewards.

. . .

You have now learned about every type of REIT on the market. Some are harder to invest in; with others, all it takes is a click of your mouse. You might think the theory behind all of this sounds great, but what if you don't have a lot of money to invest? Can you still profit with REITs if you don't have piles of cash or large amounts of disposable income?

The answer is yes.

Now, we move on to the next subject that may heavily influence your REIT investing journey: investing on a budget.

CHAPTER 7
REIT INVESTING ON A BUDGET

"In the long run, it's not just how much money you make that will determine your future prosperity. It's how much of that money you put to work by saving it and investing it."

PETER LYNCH

We're not all millionaires, and we all don't have access to limitless money. But that doesn't mean we can't change our fortunes.

If you are a first-time REIT investor or new to investing altogether, you might be starting with a modest bank account. Some people feel they don't have a chance at success if they have a shoestring budget, but that isn't the case. Don't let that fear keep you from trying and think you will never be a part of this exciting, unique investing journey.

The truth is that you *can* invest in REITs without having piles of cash. Success in REIT investing *can* happen with a limited budget. As with everything, the key is knowing how to do it.

This chapter will teach you everything you need to know about investing on a budget. It takes some work and dedication but is worth it in the long run. Years from now, when you're looking at your REIT portfolio, you'll wonder why you even had doubts.

It doesn't matter how much you start with; the main thing is starting.

On that note, let's get into some low-cost REIT investing opportunities you can capitalize on.

LOW-COST REIT INVESTMENT OPTIONS

Exchange-Traded Fund (ETF)

Let's say you want to diversify and spread your money across many REITs in different sectors, or maybe you like a few REITs in a particular sector but don't have the funds to invest in more than one. This is where ETFs are helpful.

They have flown under the radar for years but are now exploding in popularity. If you are looking for an easy way to diversify your portfolio or buy heavily in a particular sector at a fraction of the cost, then ETFs are for you.

In the most basic terms, an ETF is a way to invest in many options at once. It is a pooled investment that operates similarly to a mutual fund. However, because ETFs are bought and sold on an exchange like stocks, they are known as exchange-traded funds. An ETF typically works within a particular index, sector, or industry. It's like purchasing or investing in a group of stocks. You are buying a bundle of investments all at once, which is why they are so great, especially for new investors.

For example, let's say you want to invest in a REIT within the commercial real-estate sector but aren't sure which one to pick. You could invest in a commercial REIT ETF, exposing you to many different REITs within that sector. Or you may want to diversify. In that case, invest in an ETF holding REITs in various sectors like residential, commercial, communication towers, and retail. And they are just as easy to invest in as individual REITs since they operate the same way. They are registered on a stock exchange where anyone can buy and sell their shares. By investing in an ETF, you can save a lot of time in the research process if you plan on investing in multiple REITs. In other words, why try to find the needle when you can just buy the haystack?

A great example is the Vanguard Real Estate ETF, which I encourage you to Google to see how an ETF can provide diversification. This particular ETF holds 164 stocks across 17 different REIT types and real estate companies at the time of this writing. Imagine how long it would take to screen and evaluate that many REITs! That is the benefit of ETFs.

ETFs hold several REITs and other real estate companies, providing investors with diversified exposure to the industry and lowering risk. ETFs can even have other ETFs as part of their holdings! Talk about diversification.

Note: Regarding your screening and evaluation criteria, you may only be able to find some of the information from your 6-step process available for ETFs. However, you will always be able to find the dividend yield, which is a crucial part of your decision-making foundation. If you cannot find anything more than the dividend yield, look at the price history and risk rating to get a sense of the volatility to see if it is right for you.

. . .

Unlike most mutual funds, which only trade once daily after the markets close and are not traded on an exchange, ETFs are bought and sold throughout the day, like stocks, causing the price of the shares to fluctuate. In comparison to mutual funds, ETFs are typically cheaper and more liquid.

REITs have offered investors above-average dividend income and price growth, resulting in good overall returns. But with how many options there are, it is easy to get overwhelmed. Investors may find it challenging to select the ideal REITs for their portfolios because so many excellent options are available. By giving people extensive exposure to the top REITs, ETFs make it simple for you to participate.

Although the top holdings of most REIT ETFs are similar, the best ones each have their own distinctive approach, providing investors with a wide range of outstanding choices. REIT ETFs are great for people on a budget because it gives them plenty of options, diversification (and therefore less risk) and a way to benefit from the market without understanding it like a true expert. You will also not pay as much in fees, you will be saving time and energy, and you will still benefit from the same features that come with a REIT.

Even if you aren't on a modest budget and have considerable disposable income, ETFs have so many advantages that you would be doing yourself a disservice if you didn't look at them. REITs are about investing in multiple real estate properties at the same time, and a REIT ETF is about investing in multiple REITs at the same time. This method will help you spend less money and make a solid, educated step forward.

Note: Some real estate ETFs will strictly focus on REITs, while others will hold a combination of REITs and stock from non-REIT, real estate focused companies. There is no right or wrong answer as to which one you should invest in. If you want to invest purely in REITs, then go with an ETF that is REIT focused. If you're ok with having holdings from non-REIT, real estate related companies, go for it! It is entirely up to you and what you prefer.

EXPENSE RATIOS

This is something you'll want to pay close attention to when browsing potential ETF options. An expense ratio is how much the ETF management team charges to manage the fund. For example, if you have $1000 invested and the expense ratio is 0.50%, that means the management team takes $5 of that $1000. And it's not strictly limited to the money you invest. The expense ratio is applied on the total balance of your investment account.

Expense ratios can be as low as 0.03% or as high as 2.5%. Now, 2.5% might not seem like a big number for being at the top end, but it can significantly reduce your returns over time. For example, if you invested $100,000 and let it sit for 30 years with a 7% annual growth rate, you would end up with around $761,000. But if you pay a 2.5% expense ratio, the final number is around $374,000! That means that measly 2.5% has robbed you of around 50% of your potential growth! The little things add up.

When you're putting together a list of ETF investment opportunities, stick to the ones that have an expense ratio of 0.50% or less. The lower the better.

POPULAR REIT ETFS

What are some of the best REIT ETFs out there that you should look at when you are thinking about taking this path?

• • •

Vanguard Real Estate ETF

This is the top REIT ETF out there and with good reason. As mentioned earlier, it holds 164 stocks across 17 different REIT types and real estate sectors at the time of this writing. Investing in this ETF lets you rest easy knowing you are diversified.

The largest REITs by market size are among its top five holdings. The top two infrastructural REITs, the largest industrial REIT, and the top data center REIT are all included in this ETF.

Vanguard is known for their low expense ratios, and this ETF is no exception. With an expense ratio of just 0.12%, this ETF is easy on your bank account.

Schwab US REIT ETF

This ETF only contains REITs, as opposed to other ETFs that also buy non-REIT real estate companies, which means this ETF is purely REIT focused.

The Schwab fund owns REITs based on their market size rather than employing an equal weighting approach, like many other REIT ETFs. As a result, it shares almost all top holdings as other REIT ETFs.

Its fee structure is exceptional, which is why many people are drawn to it. Investors are able to keep more of the returns due to the ultra-low expense ratio of 0.07%.

iShares US Real Estate ETF

iShares invests in the five largest REITs and manages a variety of property types, including self-storage, industrial, data center, and telecommunications REITs.

This ETF's expense ratio of 0.40%, which is significantly higher than the industry's typical ratio, is one of its drawbacks. As a result, it has over time somewhat underperformed its benchmark since the higher charge has reduced its returns. But some people are drawn to it due to its holdings.

iShares Cohen & Steers REIT ETF

Major real estate firms that rule each of their property sectors are the main focus of this ETF. It has a focused portfolio of 30 REITs as a result.

This ETF has a comparatively higher expense ratio of 0.32% since it invests in REITs more actively. It works well for investors who wish to concentrate on the leading REITs without only looking at those in the S&P 500.

Although these ETF examples are focused on the US, you can find ETFs focusing on many different geographic locations, including Canada, the UK, Europe, etc.

PROS & CONS OF REIT ETFS

The Pros

The biggest pro is broad exposure to multiple REITs. As mentioned before, it is like getting a sampling of the best REITs on the market without having to invest in them individually. Instead, you can put your money into one ETF and you will have a taste of each of them.

A diversified income stream comes with a REIT ETF like the ones listed above. And what does diversification do for your portfolio? It helps to minimize the impacts of market fluctuations during tough times. Suppose one of your REITs is negatively impacted. In that case, only some of your investment will be hurt because you have your money in multiple pots at one time.

Also, it's just plain easier. Some people get bogged down when thinking about all the steps they need to take to invest in REITs, but by putting your money into an ETF, you are getting rid of much of the work. It's much more direct and accessible for newcomers. That is perhaps the biggest pro of them all. Too many people miss out on the exciting world of investing because they fear the work, but a REIT ETF simplifies the process.

As you can see, ETFs are particularly great for people trying to benefit from the market without spending their life savings. They may be the best option for those wanting to invest on a budget. They are also great for those just starting their investing journey and want to keep things simple.

But some cons come with REIT ETFs, too, and they must be explored before making your decision.

The Cons

One of the biggest cons comes on the back of diversification. Diversifying provides a lot more safety for your portfolio. However, it can cause you to miss out on significant financial gains too. This is because you will not be heavily invested in any given sector (unless you invest in a REIT ETF focused on a particular sector) and will only slightly capitalize on a big move from one specific sector. For example, suppose there's an explosion in price growth in commercial real estate. If you're diversified, you'll still benefit from it, but less so if you have a heavier weighting in that sector. Instead, you will rely on multiple sectors for growth, which generally fits the slow and steady approach. The more diversified you are, the safer you'll be from volatility. But volatility can also provide significant gains - and more risk. You need to find the balance that's right for you.

Fund management costs can also be a con as this can cause the performance and returns to decrease over time. When evaluating REIT ETFs, pay close attention to the expense ratios and ensure they are reasonable. You saw how big of a difference a 2.5% expense ratio can make in the long run.

Lastly, you don't have any control over the individual holdings. This may not be an issue for some people, but if you like to have complete control over what is in your portfolio, you may want to consider choosing your REITs individually.

REAL ESTATE CROWDFUNDING: THE NEW KID ON THE BLOCK

You may have heard of crowdfunding. It has become a trendy way for people to drum up grassroots support, and money, via the internet. But did you know that real estate has crowdfunding as well? It might be the key to you finding great success in REIT investing. But what is it, how does it work, and why is it so ideal for someone trying to invest on a modest budget?

Like other types of crowdfunding, real estate crowdfunding finds you pooling your money into a big pot with other people. Numerous real estate and REIT crowdfunding sites now exist, allowing newcomers to invest in the market even without any experience.

Think of it as you and your friends putting your money together to order a pizza instead of being an owner of a pizzeria. Yes, if you buy the pizza place, you can access as many pies as you want, when you want them. But suppose you put your money together with your friends and simply order pizza when you're hungry. In that case, you'll save money, still enjoy the meal, and have to devote less time, energy, and effort.

Now, it is essential to know that when doing real estate crowdfunding, you generally put all your funds into one single-property project. In that way, it is quite different from typical REITs. There are a few other things you should know before you follow the route of real estate crowdfunding.

Some pros include low minimum investment requirements, open to non-accredited investors, and the potential for significant gains if the company goes public.

Those are huge pros, right? But the biggest con of real estate crowdfunding is that you are exposed to higher risk because your money is concentrated in just one location. You can make significant money from this type of investment, but you also stand the chance of losing more because your money isn't spread out across multiple locations unless you have the funds to invest in various crowdfunding projects.

FRACTIONAL SHARES

This is one of the most exciting ways to invest on a budget!

The concept of fractional shares has only been around since 2017 (or thereabouts), so if you haven't heard of it, you're not alone.

The idea is simple; instead of only buying shares in whole numbers, you can buy fractions of shares. For example, suppose you have $100 to invest and want to buy shares of ABC REIT, but one share is worth $184. Previously, you would have had to save up the extra $84 to buy one share, but with fractional shares, you can now buy $100 worth of ABC REIT. In this example, you would own 0.54 of a share.

If you find a REIT you believe in but the share price is higher than your budget, you can still invest if fractional shares are available.

. . .

Tip: If fractional shares are something you want to include as part of your strategy, ensure the brokerage you sign up with has fractional share capability.

This chapter has shown that you have options if you aren't swimming in cash but still want to try your hand at real estate investing. The ability to invest on any budget has never been easier!

You now know almost everything needed to start your REIT investing journey, but there is something else you might be interested in; learning how to minimize your tax burden. As with all investments, there are tax implications regarding REITs. You should know how they are taxed so you can be as efficient as possible when tax time rolls around. The next chapter will teach you just that.

CHAPTER 8
HOW TO MINIMIZE YOUR TAX BURDEN

> "Today, it takes more brains and effort to make out the income-tax form than it does to make the income."
>
> ALFRED E. NEUMAN

There are few things in life that are guaranteed, and taxes are one of them.

If you are making any type of investment, you need to be aware of how it will be taxed. You simply cannot put your money into any market without the government getting a piece of the pie. That is the price of doing business and making money.

For most people, that is not a problem. Paying taxes is all part of the game, and people are willing to put up with it.

But just because it's something you must do doesn't mean you should go into it blindly. Instead, you should know the rules about how your REIT investment will be taxed. This will give you a better understanding of how it all works, of course, but it will also give you a better idea of how much money you can make in the long run after Uncle Sam gets his cut.

HOW REITS ARE TAXED

A REIT is a legal entity that, but for its unique REIT structure, would be subject to corporate taxation. But because of its unique status, it has special rules that will help you in many ways when tax time rolls around.

A company must have a significant portion of its assets and revenue in real estate to be considered a REIT. In addition, 90% of its taxable revenue must be distributed to shareholders. Due to this condition, REITs normally do not have to pay corporate income taxes and therefore won't pass the burden on to you. Nevertheless, any retained earnings would be subject to corporate tax.

It is important to know that all dividend payouts from your REIT are treated as taxable income. Therefore, the government will tax the amount of money you make from your investment every year during tax time.

The dividend may include a component denoted as a nontaxable return of capital. Return of capital means you are receiving a portion of your original investment back as income, which is technically not considered income or capital gains. If this sounds odd, rest assured that it is a standard practice in the investment world. You benefit from this by not having to pay as much tax now and deferring that cost to when you're older and most likely in a lower tax bracket.

The potential downside is that it lowers your cost base. What is a cost base? That's a fancy way of saying how much money you have invested. So, suppose you have invested

$100, and you get a return of capital of $5. Your cost base has now decreased to $95 due to the $5 return of capital. This means a larger portion of your investment will be considered capital gains. And what are capital gains? It is the increase in the value of your investment. If you invested $100 and the value has risen to $110, you have $10 in capital gains.

So, why is that a potential downside? If you hold your REIT shares long enough, there may come a point where your cost base reaches $0 and the entire value of your investment is capital gains. That means you would no longer benefit from return of capital since there would be no original investment left to return, and you would pay tax on any dividend amount. Also, if you end up selling your REIT shares, you will have to pay more capital gains tax since what you are selling is 100% capital gains.

It may sound like the tax can is just getting kicked down the road, but remember, you are in this for the long haul. One of your goals should be to hold your REIT investments long-term, so you have an income source when you retire. However, suppose you do end up selling some of your REIT shares. In that case, capital gains are taxed at a lower rate than standard income tax, so there is a silver lining!

Regarding dividends and return of capital, all of this information will be supplied to you from the REIT you are invested in via a 1099-DIV (or equivalent tax slip in your country) each tax year. Think of it like the W-2 (income slip) your job provides at the end of the year.

THE TAX ADVANTAGES OF REITS

Some people groan and complain about the idea of having to do their taxes, especially when taxed on their investments. It takes a lot of time, work, and energy, and it's never fun.

But it has to be done.

Thankfully, if you know what you are doing, you will find some tax advantages you can apply to help save some money and make the entire process far less stressful.

The most significant advantage is the pass-through deduction, which has been in effect since the 2017 Tax Cuts and Jobs Act, which was a major change to the current tax code. With it, REIT investors can deduct up to a whopping 20% of their dividends thanks to the helpful and often-used pass-through deduction. In the highest tax rate, dividend taxes for investors may decrease from 37% to 29.6%. This indicates that on $10,000 in REIT dividends, you may save up to $740 annually!

Investors choose REITs over many dividend-paying corporations mainly due to the tax advantages. As with many businesses, REITs pay dividends to investors to share revenues; however, REIT earnings are not subject to corporate tax, unlike those of many other companies, which may be passed on to investors in different ways.

The idea of depreciation is another tremendous benefit real estate investors have received from the tax code. Depreciation acts as a method of tax deferral for REITs. The likelihood that the taxable share of REIT dividends would reduce increases with the amount of depreciation expenditure. What does that mean? Some dividends are reclassified via depreciation from "ordinary income" to "return of capital." And as you just learned, return of capital means you pay less tax!

As you can see, taxes don't have to be a pain when it comes to REITs, but only if you know what to look out for.

When investing in a REIT, giving your financial records to a trusted tax consultant when tax time rolls around is best. Working on your taxes when REITs are involved can be complicated and should be taken seriously. If you are willing to learn the ins and outs of doing your taxes, by all means, forge ahead. But I will always recommend utilizing the services of someone you can trust who does taxes for a living.

Now that you know about reducing your tax burden, we can begin talking about the risks of REIT investing, which include market and interest rate risks.

CHAPTER 9
THE RISKY SIDE OF REIT INVESTING

"You can never protect yourself 100%. What you do is protect yourself as much as possible and mitigate risk to an acceptable degree. You can never remove all risk."

KEVIN MITNICK

Throughout the book, I've emphasized that any investment comes with risk. There is no way to avoid the dangers lurking in any market, but you can do things to minimize them as much as possible. The first step to reducing REIT investing risks is knowing as much about them as possible, and you're off to a great start!

While no one is perfect, you can set yourself up for a lot more success than others if you have the proper knowledge and take the suitable precautions. Remember, knowledge is power when applied correctly.

THE RISKS

Market Price

One of the biggest risks of REIT investing is something you have no control over - price movement.

The movement of the broader market will affect the bottom line of your investment and how much your REIT choice is worth. Fluctuations in the market can drastically affect your investment. When the market is strong, the value of your investment goes up. And when it's weak, your investment will suffer.

But what can you do about that? Well, the truth is that you can't do a lot. You can't control the market, and it will act like it has a mind of its own. However, you can control your emotions. The best thing you can do is stick with your investing plan and not be influenced by the market's big moves. Stay the course, and remember, eventually, everything will work out. The tough times don't last forever. Those who keep a long-term mindset and stick to their plan make the most money.

Interest Rates

Here is another risk that you have no control over. The federal government may change the interest rate, and when it does, that could impact your REIT investment.

This applies more so to those who have put their money into a mortgage REIT. Remember in Chapter 2 when we reviewed the impact of rates on mortgage REITs? Mortgage REITs could do well when rates increase, or they could suffer. It all depends on how the REIT has structured their portfolio.

When the Fed wants to adjust interest rates, it will do so without concern for your investments. Again, the best thing to do is stay the course when this occurs. The worst thing you can do is abandon your REIT when the environment isn't ideal.

That being said, all REITs are affected by interest rates to a degree. During periods of economic growth, REIT prices tend to rise along with interest rates for a duration of time. The reason is that a growing economy increases the value of REITs because the value of their underlying real estate assets increases. In a growing economy, the demand for financing also increases, resulting in increased interest rates.

However, in a slowing economy, the relationship turns negative when the Fed tightens the money supply and keeps going up, up, up. In these situations, investors typically opt for US Treasuries, which are government-guaranteed, with most paying a fixed interest rate. As a result, when rates rise during tightening, REITs tend to sell off and the bond market rallies as investment capital flows into bonds. If this happens, remember to control your emotions and stick to your plan.

Tip: Pay attention to the economy and what the government's stance is on interest rates. You will be able to see rate changes coming and can prepare, making it less of a shock when the market reacts.

Liquidity Risk

As you learned earlier, certain types of REITs are less liquid. Non-traded REITs fall into this risk category, and you may be unable to get your money out when needed. This is why I recommend investing in publicly traded REITs. They are highly liquid.

Credit Risk

Credit risk is directly tied to the person or business paying a mortgage. Suppose a borrower defaults and stops making their monthly payments. That's an issue. Particularly for mortgage REITs since they rely on those payments to make a profit. Again, this impacts mortgage REITs more so.

Investor Risk

Now, here is a type of risk that you *do* have some influence over.

Every investor's worst enemy is themselves. You hold the power to decide if you will be successful or not. If you don't make properly informed choices, you are setting yourself up to fail. But if you take the time to learn, make a plan, and follow it, you are setting yourself up for great financial success.

Investor risk is entirely in your hands. Again, this all goes back to what we discussed a few chapters ago: doing the work that comes with investing and creating a plan you believe in and can follow. This will take time and effort, but it is worth it. With the sheer number of resources we have access to in the modern age, there is no excuse for making poorly informed choices and exposing yourself to unnecessary investor risk. You must ensure you make the right investment choice that fits you and then do everything you can to stick to your chosen plan.

Many investors rush the process and make the wrong decisions. Sure, you can bounce back, but it will add more time and effort to the process. Every time you deviate from the plan, you tack on additional time and energy to get yourself back on track.

As you know, risks are part of life. The world will keep spinning, and the industries affecting your investment will continue forging ahead. You can't avoid all the risks, but you can be aware of them.

Something else to be mindful of that ties into risk are the dos and don'ts of REIT investing, which you'll discover in the next chapter, and will wrap the bow around everything you have learned up to this point.

CHAPTER 10
DOS AND DON'TS OF REIT INVESTING

"It's the little details that are vital. Little things make big things happen."

JOHN WOODEN

So far, you have seen how straightforward it is to invest in REITs. But there are still a few things you'll want to keep in mind before you make any investment decisions. You have learned a lot about what a REIT is, how it works, the differences between the various types, the things to look for when choosing the right one for you, and the risks.

But to be a successful, consistent, and happy investor, you also need to understand the nuances of the market beyond the basics. And that means that you need to understand the dos and don'ts of REIT investing.

Some of these may be refreshers, but they are important nonetheless.

Do: Think Long-Term

Investing requires commitment. Consider that you will be holding this investment for years or even decades. If you want to turn a profit quickly, you will be disappointed. But if you are willing to commit to a long-term mindset, create a plan, and stick with it, you will be successful.

Remember, consistency over time wins.

Do: Focus On Total Return, Not Just Yield

Some people think REITs solely are ways to make income from an investment, so they look for a good yield, ignore any potential price growth, and call it a day. But this isn't the right approach. The smarter move is to focus instead on the total return you may eventually make. In other words, you need to look at the potential price growth for the REIT on top of the yield. Why? Because REITs often outperform stocks in terms of price-performance! Don't start this journey with a one-track mind. Instead, look at the historical price growth and determine the potential total return you might eventually make if you hold steady and follow your plan.

Tip: Remember the concept of DRIP (dividend reinvestment plans)? If you invest in a REIT that has excellent price growth and use a DRIP, you will create a price growth loop. Dividends automatically buy more shares, shares grow in value and provide higher dividend payouts, those payouts get reinvested and the loop starts all over again.

Do: Diversify

Focusing on the power of diversification when you are investing in REITs is essential. In other words, don't put all your eggs in one basket. The more you spread out your money, the better your chance of a solid financial future. This also means you'll have less risk. Remember, if your money is in several different places simultaneously, you lower the impact of the rough times in specific real estate sectors and the risk of losing everything.

Do: Pay Attention to Foreign Markets

So many people are close-minded when it comes to REITs. They think the country they live in has the only market worth investing in and don't expand their horizons beyond it.

The truth is that there are many different REITs from all over the globe, all related to various real estate markets that are brimming with potential. Just because you don't live in a particular country doesn't mean you can't profit from it. Pay attention to the UK, Canada, Asia, Europe and beyond. You may be surprised that investing in them is relatively easy and can add a lot to your bottom line.

Don't: Pay Too much Attention To Quarterly Results

Quarterly results will give you a small sampling of how well your REIT is doing, but these shouldn't be the results you pay the closest attention to. If you put too much weight on them, you will find yourself making brash, quick decisions based only on the last few months of data. Quarterly results are just a snapshot of how well your REIT investments are doing; they do not tell the whole tale.

Again, this is a long-term commitment. You have to consider the big picture when investing in REITs.

Don't: Skip Due Diligence

You are well aware of this concept by now, but I will mention it one more time to illustrate just how important it is.

Unfortunately, too many investors believe money will equal success in the REIT market. But that could not be further from the truth. The truth is you need to invest that money wisely, in the sort of REITs that have the potential for long-term success. And that means that you will have to do the work. You will need to put in the time and effort to make sure you choose REITs wisely and not pick something just because it's shiny and exciting.

You must be a smart investor. You must learn, apply knowledge and have determination. And all of this has to be done before you choose to invest. If you are going to throw your money around without making a sound choice, you might as well go to the casino.

Don't: Hesitate

Hesitating can lead you down the path of analysis paralysis. Overthinking will cause you to second-guess yourself and your decisions, which may cause you to miss out on a lucrative price move. If you find a REIT that fits your criteria and feel confident investing, make your move. Of course, do your research and stick with dollar cost averaging, but don't hesitate for too long or you might talk yourself out of investing altogether.

Don't: Time the Market

Trying to time the market is one of the surest ways to lose money. Sure, you might get lucky a few times, but it is a losing proposition in the long run. Trying to time the market with buying low and selling high isn't investing; it's day trading. While you might think you are outsmarting the market and other investors, timing the market is a losing game, and you are not here to play games with your hard-earned money, right?

And finally, remember that REITs are companies at the end of the day. They aren't guaranteed money-making machines; there is a human element to them, which is why you need to look at management before investing in one. The management team can help a REIT take flight or run it into the ground. Make sure you know *who* you are investing in as well as what you are investing in.

There are many tricks of the trade you will pick up along the way. You may be a newcomer now, but in the years ahead, you will become fluent in REIT investing. If you have a desire to continually learn, you will find that investing becomes easier, more enjoyable, and more success will come your way.

Now that you have learned the basics, it's time to move on to advanced REIT investing strategies.

CHAPTER 11
ADVANCED REIT STRATEGIES

"If you are not willing to learn, no one can help you. If you are determined to learn, no one can stop you."

ZIG ZIGLAR

A day will come when you find the foundational methods you have learned are second nature. When that day comes, you may want more advanced strategies to take your REIT investing to the next level.

It might be some time before you get to the point where you are using this advice, but it's important nonetheless.

REIT OPTION TRADING

If you have ever gone down the investing rabbit hole, you may have stumbled across options and learned how they can help hedge a portfolio against risk, minimize potential losses and even increase profitability. REIT option trading is just one of the many advanced strategies professionals use.

If options are a new concept to you, that's ok! You are going to learn everything you need to know so you can utilize them in your strategy.

Contracts known as options provide the holder the right, but not the obligation, to purchase or sell a certain quantity of an underlying asset at a specified price at or before the contract expiration. You will often hear the specified price referred to as a strike price.

There are two types of options - call options and put options. When you buy a call option, you will make money if the price of a stock, or REIT in our case, goes up. When you buy a put option, you will make money if the price goes down.

Here is an example of what this means: REIT ABC is trading at $50 per share, and you think the price will rise. You buy a call option with a strike price of $55. Let's say the price of REIT ABC rises to $65. You can exercise your call option and buy shares of REIT ABC for $55 since that is the option's strike price, even though the current price is $65 per share. You now instantly have $10 of profit per share, which you can collect if you sell the shares. Or you can hold the shares if you think they will appreciate even further.

Since options have value themselves, you could also sell the option and pocket any profit you have made. Sticking with our example of a $55 strike price, the higher the price of REIT ABC goes above $55, the more your call option is worth.

So, how much does it cost to buy an option? That depends on a few things.

Each option has a premium attached to it, which is the price you pay for the option. For our call option example on REIT ABC, if the premium is $500, you are paying $500 for that option. However, the premium fluctuates based on the underlying asset's price (REIT ABC). If the price of REIT ABC rises above a given strike price, a call option's premium will increase. If the price of REIT ABC declines, a call option's premium will decrease. This concept is often called "in the money" or "out of the money." Sticking with our REIT ABC example, since our strike price is $55 and the share price is $65, our call option is in the money by $10. The further your option is in the money, the more the premium will increase, increasing your potential profit if you sell the option. However, if the price of REIT ABC is $50 and the call option has a strike of $55, the option is out of the money by $5.

Something else that affects an option's premium is how many people are buying it. The more interest in an option, the more the premium will rise.

Also, options are available for many different strike prices. REIT ABC could have options available at $1 intervals. For example, options could be available at strike prices of $50, $51, $52, etc. However, the closer your strike price is to the share price of the underlying asset, the more expensive the premium will be.

Options also have expiration dates. As this date gets closer, the option's value decreases, affecting the premium and how much you can sell it for. This is known as time decay. If your option is in the money, the value will increase, but only for so long. Once the expiration date gets close, the value will start to drop. Suppose you don't sell it or exercise it before the expiration date. In that case, it will expire worthless, therefore losing the premium you paid.

Strike prices and expiration dates make buying and selling options a balancing act. You want to buy an option with an expiration date far enough away to give the underlying asset price enough time to move in the given direction of your strike price.

Now, it is essential to know that options are more of a

short-term, complementary strategy, and less about long-term investing. It takes much more time to monitor and execute option strategies, which can sometimes get complex. But if you want to take the time to learn about them, they can provide major benefits.

If you want to incorporate options into your overall strategy, take the time to learn more about them, as this is a very surface-level crash course. You need to understand them on a deeper level to utilize them appropriately. This is an advanced strategy that requires advanced learning. Entire books have been written on the subject and there are many to choose from!

Now that you have learned the basics of options, I'm sure you are starting to see their value and how you can use them in your strategy. They can be valuable hedging tools to provide some security in your portfolio, limit potential losses, and even increase profitability.

However, I want to emphasize that you can leave options out of your investing strategy! *They are not essential to your success.* Remember, consistency over time is what wins.

200-DAY MOVING AVERAGE

The 200-day moving average is the average closing price of a stock over the last 200 days. This average is typically used to determine the long-term trend for a stock and whether it is a good time to invest, and it can also be used for REITs.

If the current share price is above the 200-day moving average, it is considered bullish (price will most likely go up) and has a better chance of increasing in value. However, suppose it is below the 200-day moving average. In that case, it is considered bearish (price will most likely go down), which gives it a higher probability of declining.

The slope of the moving average should also be taken into

consideration. If the moving average is sloping upwards, that is a bullish signal. If the slope is downward, that is a bearish signal. It is generally best to have the price action and slope of the moving average both bullish or bearish. For example, suppose the share price of a REIT is above an upward-sloping 200-day moving average. In that case, that is a strong indicator that the price of the REIT will continue to rise. The opposite would be true as an indicator of a stock price continuing to decline.

Now that you understand the theory behind this tool, it's time to use it! You'll need to use an online charting website for this to be effective, such as barchart.com.

Go to barchart.com and search for a REIT you're interested in. If you don't have a list of potential REITs to invest in yet, use Realty Income Corp as an example. When the information page loads, click on the "Full Chart" button to open the full-size chart. Click on the "+Study" button near the top of the chart, select "Moving Average" from the list, and set the "Period" to 200. There you have it! You can now compare the current REIT price to the 200-day moving average.

Here is a an example screenshot so you can see what a chart will look like with the 200-day moving average applied:

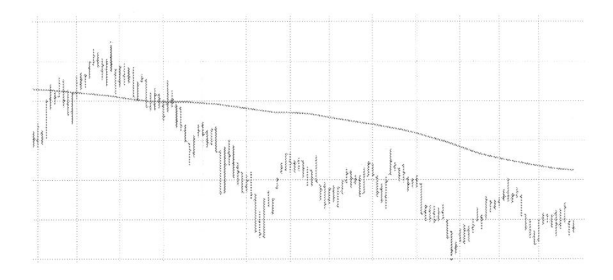

As you can see, the price is below a downward-sloping 200-day moving average, which is a strong, bearish signal. Once the 200-day moving average starts to slope upward and the REIT price breaks above it, that's a signal that things may be turning around.

So, what can you use the 200-day moving average for? For example, if you see a REIT starting a strong, bullish trend, you could theoretically increase your monthly contributions for a period of time to capitalize on the upward price movement. Then, go back to your regular contribution amount once the trend is over. However, like any metric, it shouldn't be the only thing you base your decisions on. It's one tool to help you see the bigger picture.

And just like options, you can leave this out of your investing strategy. *It is not essential to your success!* Remember, consistency over time is what wins.

USING LEVERAGE

If you see a fantastic opportunity to invest in a REIT but need more cash on hand, or want to invest a larger sum, taking out a loan to invest is an option. But I want to be clear that using debt to invest carries its own set of risks. The primary risk being you have a monthly payment you need to make, which eats into your income, and can affect your regular investment schedule. Additionally, if you haven't done proper due diligence and your investment tanks, you now have a loan with no assets to offset it.

You also need to think about interest rates when considering this option. If rates increase, you may be in a situation where you have a monthly payment you can't afford.

Using leverage can accelerate your results, but you should only consider it if you have done extreme due diligence on the potential REIT investment, as well as your personal finances. Can you comfortably survive a worst-case scenario? Think about how it will affect the people around you and not just yourself.

RELATIONSHIP TO YOUR EXISTING INVESTMENTS

If you have an existing investment portfolio, you will also want to consider how REITs will affect it. Are your potential REIT investments in related industries or sectors of your current investments? Or do they provide diversification in your overall portfolio?

Suppose you have investments in a related industry to the REIT you are wanting to invest in. In that case, you may want to reconsider buying it. Having too many positively correlated assets can substantially increase risk.

At the end of the day, your success in REIT investing is all about knowing yourself, what you want, what you wish to avoid, and the level of commitment and energy you're willing to put into it. You need to have an honest conversation with yourself before you can create a long-term, healthy strategy for your future in REIT investing.

And that's it. You have made it to the end of the book! You have come a long way, learned a lot, and created an image of the sort of REIT investor you want to be.

But don't go away yet, because the book isn't quite finished. Ahead are some closing words that reflect on everything you learned and will set you on your path to REIT success.

CHAPTER 12
CONCLUSION

"Whether you think you can or you think you can't, you're right."

HENRY FORD

You now have the knowledge and tools to invest in REITs confidently. Using what you have learned, you can now move forward with the ability to know what you want and how to get it. You know the sort of investor you want to be, the risks to avoid, and the pitfalls that often catch people off guard and send them down the wrong path.

As with anything, your chances of success with REITs all hinge upon the amount of time, energy, and effort you put into it. How seriously will you take this? Success is there, waiting for you to reach out and grab it.

The great news is that you can start investing as soon as possible. In fact, you can start today. Getting started is easy.

Open a brokerage account, do your research, create a plan, and start your REIT portfolio.

As you go through the process outlined in this book, always keep in mind that knowledge is the key. If it feels overwhelming or complicated at times, remember that at the core of all success is the desire to learn and become an expert. It will get easier. Those who are good at investing - or anything for that matter - don't sit back and let the world pass them by. They are proactive, they are driven, and they are determined to keep learning.

Even seasoned investors don't learn enough about REITs and the power they hold. That means there are millions of people missing out on the benefits they provide. But you don't have to be one of them.

If you want to make REITs worth your time, you must treat this as more than a hobby or something you do in your spare time. Instead, treat it like a job. Or, better yet, treat it like something that can help you attain financial freedom.

Remember to research and look at your options for Equity, Mortgage, and Hybrid REITs to determine which is best for you. There are many types of REITs belonging to several different industries, including healthcare, self-storage, hospitality, offices, and more. There is a REIT - or REIT ETF - for everyone; you just need to put in the time to find it.

As you have seen, there is much to gain from REITs. They are fantastic opportunities that typically outperform traditional investments, provide solid income streams, and are considered lower risk than many other investment types.

This book is just the start of your journey. You will continue to learn along the way and fine-tune your approach. Remember, when the challenging times come, stick to your plan and maintain your long-term mindset.

My aim is to teach you how to generate wealth from real estate without owning physical property; I hope I did just that. You *can* reap the rewards of real estate without buying and managing properties. All it takes is the time and effort to learn how.

Welcome to the new age of real estate. Welcome to getting rich with REIT investing.

If you enjoyed this book and found what you learned helpful, please hop on Amazon and leave a review! It will help others find this book and, in turn, help them learn how to benefit from the fantastic world of REITs.

REFERENCES

A beginner's guide to private REITs. (2022). *www.yieldstreet.com*. https://www.yieldstreet.com/resources/article/beginner-guide-to-private-reits/

Admin. (2022). Investment Fees Calculator. *Ativa Interactive Corp*. https://ativa.com/investment-fees-calculator/

Advantages to investing in real estate investment trusts. (n.d.). https://www.managementstudyguide.com/real-estate-investment-trusts-advantages.htm

Bovaird, C. (2022). REIT ETFs provide investors with an easy way to gain broad access to the real estate market. *Business Insider*. https://www.businessinsider.com/personal-finance/what-is-a-reit-etf

Bowler, D. (2021, March 2). REIT Management Matters - How To Pick The Right Ones. *Seeking Alpha*. https://seekingalpha.com/article/4391795-reit-management-matters-how-to-pick-right-ones

Bryant, S. (2022). REITs vs. Real Estate Crowdfunding. *Investopedia*. https://www.investopedia.com/articles/personal-finance/071015/reits-vs-real-estate-crowdfunding-how-they-differ.asp

Cazzin, J. (2023, February 3). FP Answers: What are REITs and how do they fit into a balanced portfolio? *Financialpost*. https://financialpost.com/investing/reits-fit-balanced-portfolio

Cfp, M. F. (2023a). How to value a REIT. *The Motley Fool*. https://www.fool.com/investing/stock-market/market-sectors/real-estate-investing/reit/how-to-value-reit/#:~:text=REITs%20tend%20to%20have%20higher,could%20be%20on%20the%20horizon

Cfp, M. F. (2023b). How to value a REIT. *The Motley Fool*. https://www.fool.com/investing/stock-market/market-sectors/real-estate-investing/reit/how-to-value-reit/

Chen, J. (2021). Dividend Per Share (DPS) Definition and Formula. *Investopedia*. https://www.investopedia.com/terms/d/dividend-per-share.asp

Chen, J. (2023a). Blind Pool: Overview, benefits, criticisms. *Investopedia*. https://www.investopedia.com/terms/b/blind_pool.asp#:~:text=A%20blind%20pool%2C%20also%20known,that%20are%20raised%20from%20investors

Chen, J. (2023b). Funds from Operations (FFO): a way to measure REIT performance. *Investopedia.* https://www.investopedia.com/terms/f/fundsfromoperation.asp

Choosing the right REIT. (n.d.). RegionsBank. https://www.regions.com/insights/wealth/taxes-and-estate-planning/planning-tax-strategies/choosing-the-right-reit

Cussen, M. P. (2021). The basics of REIT taxation. *Investopedia.* https://www.investopedia.com/articles/pf/08/reit-tax.asp

DiLallo, M. (2023a). Investing in mortgage REITs. *The Motley Fool.* https://www.fool.com/investing/stock-market/market-sectors/real-estate-investing/reit/mortgage-reit/

DiLallo, M. (2023b). Investing in REIT ETFs. *The Motley Fool.* https://www.fool.com/investing/stock-market/market-sectors/real-estate-investing/reit/reit-etf/

DiLallo, M. (2023c). REITs vs. Stocks: Everything You Need to Know. *The Motley Fool.* https://www.fool.com/research/reits-vs-stocks/

Dividend.com. (n.d.-a). Dividend.com. https://www.dividend.com/how-to-invest/traded-versus-non-traded-reits/#:~:text=Non%2Dtraded%20REITs%20are%20similarly,on%20the%20real%20estate%20market

Dividend.com. (n.d.-b). Dividend.com. https://www.dividend.com/how-to-invest/traded-versus-non-traded-reits/

Downey, L. (2023). Essential Options Trading Guide. *Investopedia.* https://www.investopedia.com/options-basics-tutorial-4583012

Farley, A. (2023a). How to Assess REITs Using Funds from Operations (FFO/AFFO). *Investopedia.* https://www.investopedia.com/investing/how-to-assess-real-estate-investment-trust-reit/

Farley, A. (2023b). How to Assess REITs Using Funds from Operations (FFO/AFFO). *Investopedia.* https://www.investopedia.com/investing/how-to-assess-real-estate-investment-trust-reit/#:~:text=Investors%20who%20want%20to%20estimate,funds%20from%20operations%20(FFO

Financial benefits of REITs. (n.d.). Nareit. https://www.reit.com/investing/financial-benefits-reits#:~:text=REITs%20offer%20investors%20the%20benefits,inflation%20protection%20and%20portfolio%20diversi

Folger, J. (2021). Direct Real Estate Investing vs. REITs. *Investopedia.* https://www.investopedia.com/articles/investing/072314/investing-real-estate-versus-reits.asp

Foxcraft, & Foxcraft. (2021). Rick Kahler: Don't gamble on private REITs I Kahler Financial. *Kahler Financial I Financial Planners, Rapid City, SD.* https://kahlerfinancial.com/financial-awakenings/weekly-column/private-reits-not-a-good-choice-for-small-investors

Fundrise. (n.d.). https://fundrise.com/education/reits-101-a-beginners-guide-to-real-estate-investment-trusts

Gerstein, M. (2018a, July 5). Screening For High-Yielding High-Quality

REITs. *Forbes.* https://www.forbes.com/sites/marcgerstein/2018/07/05/screening-for-high-yielding-high-quality-reits/?sh=79100d4f2a07

Gerstein, M. (2018b, July 5). Screening For High-Yielding High-Quality REITs. *Forbes.* https://www.forbes.com/sites/marcgerstein/2018/07/05/screening-for-high-yielding-high-quality-reits/?sh=7132d3f12a07

Guide to Equity REIT Investing. (n.d.). Nareit. https://www.reit.com/what-reit/types-reits/guide-equity-reits#:~:text=What%20are%20Equity%20REITs%3F,lease%20the%20space%20to%20tenants

Guide to Mortgage REIT (MREIT) Investing. (n.d.). Nareit. https://www.reit.com/what-reit/types-reits/guide-mortgage-reits

Guide to Public Non-Listed REIT (PNLR) Investing. (n.d.). Nareit. https://www.reit.com/what-reit/types-reits/guide-public-non-listed-reits-pnlrs

Hall, J. (2023). Non-traded REITs vs. Traded REITs. *The Motley Fool.* https://www.fool.com/investing/stock-market/market-sectors/real-estate-investing/reit/non-traded-vs-traded-reits/

Hargrave, M. (2023). Net Asset Value Per Share (NAVPS): Definition, Formula, Uses. *Investopedia.* https://www.investopedia.com/terms/n/navpershare.asp

Harper, D. R. (2022). How to analyze REITs (Real Estate Investment Trusts). *Investopedia.* https://www.investopedia.com/articles/04/030304.asp#toc-how-to-analyze-reits

Hawrylack, S. (n.d.). *REIT tax advantages.* https://www.concreit.com/blog/reit-tax-advantages#:~:text=Why%20Are%20REITs%20Tax%20Efficient,the%20qualified%20business%20income%20deduction

Hayes, A. (2021). Return of Capital (ROC): what it is, how it works, and examples. *Investopedia.* https://www.investopedia.com/terms/r/returnofcapital.asp#:~:text=Key%20Takeaways,investment%20accounts%20return%20gains%20first

How higher interest rates impact REITs. (2018, January 1). World of Dividends by Simply Safe Dividends. https://www.simplysafedividends.com/world-of-dividends/posts/20-how-higher-interest-rates-impact-reits

How I select the best Real Estate Investment Trusts (REITs). (2023, May 22). https://marcoschwartz.com/how-i-select-the-best-real-estate-investment-trusts-reits

How to find the best Real Estate Investment Trusts (REITs). (n.d.). https://dividenddetective.com/screen_for_reits.htm#:~:text=Finding%20REITs,all%20of%20the%20available%20filters

How to form a Real Estate Investment Trust (REIT). (n.d.). Nareit.

https://www.reit.com/what-reit/how-form-reit#:~:text=Quarterly%2C%20at%20least%2075%25%20of,loans%20secured%20by%20real%20propert

Karsh, J., & Karsh, J. (2022). REIT tax Advantages - Streitwise. *Streitwise.* https://streitwise.com/reit-tax-advantages/

Law, J. (2019, March 13). How Tax Efficient Are Your REITs? *Seeking Alpha.* https://seekingalpha.com/article/4248434-how-tax-efficient-are-your-reits

Maverick, J. (2022). Is NAV the best way to assess the value of a REIT? *Investopedia.* https://www.investopedia.com/ask/answers/020615/nav-best-way-assess-value-reit.asp#:~:text=The%20market%20value%20minus%20any,deprecation%20is%20%2410%2C000%20a%20year

Merrill, T., & Merrill, T. (2021a). What are mortgage REITs? a real estate investor's guide. *FortuneBuilders.* https://www.fortunebuilders.com/mortgage-reits/

Merrill, T., & Merrill, T. (2021b). REIT Investing: A Guide For Beginners & Real Estate Investors. *FortuneBuilders.* https://www.fortunebuilders.com/reit-investing/

Moskowitz, D. (2022). What are the risks of real Estate Investment Trusts (REITs)? *Investopedia.* https://www.investopedia.com/articles/investing/031915/what-are-risks-reits.asp#toc-risks-of-non-traded-reits

Nickolas, S. (2023). Equity REIT vs. Mortgage REIT. *Investopedia.* https://www.investopedia.com/ask/answers/052815/what-difference-between-equity-reit-and-mortgage-reit.asp#toc-equity-reits

RealWealth. (2022, May 18). *10 Real estate Goals for SMART & Lucrative Investing.* https://realwealth.com/learn/10-real-estate-goals-smart-lucrative-investing/

REIT Institute. (2019, June 8). *REITs vs Real Estate Options - REIT Institute.* https://www.reitinstitute.com/reits-vs-real-estate-options/

REIT Valuation Methods | Tutorial Guide + Examples. (2023, June 27). Wall Street Prep. https://www.wallstreetprep.com/knowledge/reit-valuation-4-most-common-approaches-used-in-practice/

REITs by the numbers. (n.d.). Nareit. https://www.reit.com/data-research/data/reits-numbers

Reitscompass. (2019a, September 17). REITs Valuation: Price to book ratio. *reitscompass.* https://www.reitscompass.com/post/reits-valuation-price-to-book-ratio#:~:text=A%20price%20to%20book%20ratio,high%20risk%20with%20possible%20correction

Reitscompass. (2019b, September 17). REITs Valuation: Price to book ratio. *reitscompass.* https://www.reitscompass.com/post/reits-valuation-price-to-book-ratio#:~:text=PB%20is%20a%20ratio%20that,twice%20its%20NAV%20per%20share

Rental Software. (2015, November 24). *Real estate Definitions: Return on equity*

(ROE) real estate. Real Estate Investment Software. https://www.rentalsoftware.com/return-on-equity-real-estate/#:~:text=Cash%2Don%2D-Cash%20Return%20is,%2Don%2DCash%20Return%20calculation

Risk factors. (n.d.). https://www.prospectrm.com/en/about-reit/risk-factors

Risk factors | REITAS – REIT Association of Singapore. (n.d.). https://www.reitas.sg/reit-basics/risk-factors-to-consider-when-investing-in-a-reit/

SEC.gov | Accredited Investor. (2022, March 26). https://www.sec.gov/education/capitalraising/building-blocks/accredited-investor

Seth, S. (2022). Are REITs beneficial during a High-Interest era? *Investopedia*. https://www.investopedia.com/articles/investing/091615/are-reits-beneficial-during-highinterest-era.asp

SMART goals for your financial plan. (n.d.). Schwab Brokerage. https://www.schwab.com/learn/story/smart-goals-your-financial-plan

Staff, A. (2022). REIT Taxation Basics. *The Motley Fool*. https://www.fool.com/the-ascent/taxes/reit-taxation-basics/

Staff, M. F. (2022). What is a hybrid REIT? *The Motley Fool*. https://www.fool.com/investing/stock-market/market-sectors/real-estate-investing/reit/hybrid-reit/

Suknanan, J. (2021, December 2). 145 million Americans own REITs: 12 things to know about these stocks that make owning real estate easy. *CNBC*. https://www.cnbc.com/select/what-to-know-about-reits/

Team, C. (2023a). Risk factors of investing in REITs. *Corporate Finance Institute*. https://corporatefinanceinstitute.com/resources/capital-markets/risk-factors-of-investing-in-reits/

Team, C. (2023b). Risk factors of investing in REITs. *Corporate Finance Institute*. https://corporatefinanceinstitute.com/resources/capital-markets/risk-factors-of-investing-in-reits/

Team, I. (2021). The REIT way. *Investopedia*. https://www.investopedia.com/articles/03/013103.asp#toc-picking-the-right-reit

Team, I. (2022a). REITs vs. REIT ETFs: How They Compare. *Investopedia*. https://www.investopedia.com/articles/investing/081415/reits-vs-reit-etfs-how-they-compare.asp#:~:text=REIT%20exchange%2Dtraded%20-funds%20invest,mortgage%20REITs%2C%20and%20hybrid%20REITs

Team, I. (2022b). Real estate crowdfunding: Meaning, pros and cons, limitations. *Investopedia*. https://www.investopedia.com/ask/answers/100214/what-real-estate-crowdfunding.asp#:~:text=1-,Advantages,a%20small%20amount%20of%20cash

The most important metrics for REIT investing. (2018, January 1). World of Dividends by Simply Safe Dividends. https://www.simplysafedividends.com/world-of-dividends/posts/21-the-most-important-metrics-for-reit-investing

The role of real estate investments in a portfolio. (2023, January 11). Morningstar,

Inc. https://www.morningstar.com/articles/1131921/the-role-of-real-estate-investments-in-a-portfolio

The Tokenist. (2023, January 9). *REITs vs. Stocks Comparison (2023) - The Tokenist*. Tokenist. https://tokenist.com/investing/reits-vs-stocks/

Twin, A. (2022). What is risk tolerance, and why does it matter? *Investopedia*. https://www.investopedia.com/terms/r/risktolerance.asp#:~:text=Risk%20tolerance%20is%20the%20degree,investments%20that%20an%20individual%20chooses

Wealth, S. (2023). Skyline Wealth Explains: Public vs Private Real Estate Investment Trusts (REITs). *Skyline Wealth*. https://skylinewealth.ca/articles/skyline-wealth-explains-public-vs-private-reits/

What's a REIT (Real Estate Investment Trust)? (n.d.). Nareit. https://www.reit.com/what-reit

Yahoo is part of the Yahoo family of brands. (n.d.). https://finance.yahoo.com/news/4-high-yield-reits-low-160344596.html#:~:text=The%20payout%20ratio%20is%20derived,above%2075%25%20are%20considered%20unsafe

Printed in Great Britain
by Amazon

2cda3586-a5f2-4832-bdfd-3ee07502de02R01